THE
LIFE AND CHARACTER

OF THE LATE REVEREND, LEARNED, AND PIOUS

MR. JONATHAN EDWARDS

PRESIDENT OF THE COLLEGE OF NEW JERSEY

TOGETHER WITH

Extracts from his Private Writings & Diary

By

Samuel Hopkins

Appendices by Esther Burr the daughter of Mr. Edwards.

Foreword by the Editor H. Rondel Rumburg

~~~~~~

The righteous shall be in everlasting remembrance, Psalm 112:6.

~~~~~~

Harrisonburg, Virginia
SPRINKLE PUBLICATIONS
2008

This edition of *The Life and Character of the Late Reverend, Learned, and Pious Mr. Jonathan Edwards,* was originally published at Northampton, and printed by Andrew Wright, for S. & E. Butler, 1804.

The Sprinkle Publications edition was newly typeset and updated by Dr. H. Rondel Rumburg of the Society for Biblical and Southern Studies in 2008.

SPRINKLE PUBLICATIONS
PO Box 1094
Harrisonburg, Virginia 22803

© 2008

ISBN #978-1-59442-161-7

PREFACE

𝔓RESIDENT EDWARDS, in the esteem of all the judicious, who were well acquainted with him, either personally or by his writings, was one of the *greatest* ... *best* ... and *most useful* of men that have lived in this age.

He discovered himself to be one of the *greatest of divines* by his conversation, preaching and writings: one of remarkable strength of mind, clearness of thought and depth of penetration, who well understood, and was able, above most others, to vindicate the great doctrines of Christianity.

And no one perhaps has been in our day more universally esteemed and acknowledged to be a *bright Christian*, an eminently *good man*. His love to God and man; his zeal for God and his cause; his uprightness, humility, self-denial and weanedness from the world; his close walk with God; his conscientious, constant and universal obedience, in all exact and holy ways of living: in one word, the goodness, the holiness of his heart, has been as evident and conspicuous, as the uncommon greatness and strength of his understanding.

And that this distinguished light has not shone in vain, there are a cloud of witnesses. God, who gave him his great talents, led him into a way of improving them, both by preaching and writing, which has doubtless proved the means of converting many from the error of their ways; and of greatly promoting the interest of Christ's church, both in America and Europe. And there is reason to hope, that though he is now dead, he will yet speak for a great while to come, to the great comfort and advantage of the church of Christ; that his publications will produce a yet greater harvest, as an addition to his joy and crown of rejoicing in the day of the Lord.

But the design of the following memoirs is not merely to publish these things, and tell the world how eminently great, wise, holy and useful President Edwards was; but rather to inform in what way, and by what means, he attained to such an uncommon stock of knowledge and holiness; and how, in the improvement of this, he did so much good to mankind; that others may hereby be directed and excited to go and do likewise.

The reader is, therefore, not to expect a mere encomium on the dead, but a faithful and plain narration of matters of fact, together with his own internal exercise expressed in his own words; and is desired not to look on the following composure so much an act of friendship to the dead, as of kindness to the living; it being only an attempt to render a life that has been greatly useful, yet more so. And as this is designed for the reader's good, he is desired to remember, that if he gets no benefit hereby is not made wiser nor better, gains no skill or disposition to live an holy and useful life, all is in vain to him.

In this world, so full of darkness and delusion, it is of great importance, that all should be able to distinguish between true religion and that which is false. In this, perhaps, none has taken more pains or labored more successfully than he whose life is set before the reader. And it is presumed that his religious resolutions, exercises and conduct here exhibited, will serve well to exemplify and illustrate all that he has written on this subject. Here pure and undefiled religion, in distinction from all counterfeits, appears in life and practice, exhibiting a picture which will tend to instruct, strengthen and comfort all those, who, in their religious sentiments and exercises, are built on the foundation of the Apostles and Prophets, of which Jesus Christ is the chief cornerstone; while their hearts and practices, in some measure, answer to it, as in water, face answers to face. And here, they who have hitherto

5

unhappily been in darkness and delusion, in this infinitely important affair, may have matter of instruction and conviction.

This is a point about which, above many others, the Protestant world is in the dark and needs instruction, as Mr. Edwards was more and more convinced the longer he lived; and which he was wont frequently to observe in conversation. If, therefore, these his remains are adapted to answer this end, and may be considered as a word behind all to whom they shall come, "saying, THIS IS THE WAY, walk ye in it," and shall in this view, be blessed to many, it will be a relief under one of the greatest calamities that attend the Christian world, and promote that important end, so worthy the attention and pursuit of all; and in which he, from whom this mantle falls, was zealously engaged, and which he pursued to the end of his life.

In this view, especially, is the following life offered to the public, with an earnest desire, that every reader may faithfully improve it to this purpose; while he candidly overlooks any improprieties and defects which he may observe to be chargeable on the compiler; who is, he knows, in a great degree unequal to what is here attempted.

August 20, 1764

FOREWORD

Hopkins' pen was pure gold and flowed in a stream of accuracy in depicting the very essence of Jonathan Edwards' person. His succinctness may be found in the following example. Edwards "took his religious principles from the Bible, and not from any human system or body of divinity. Though his principles were *Calvinistic*, yet he called no man father. He thought and judged for himself, and was truly very much of an original. This is evident by what he published in his life time, and is yet more so by his manuscripts." Here Hopkins evidences a genuine understanding of his subject!

~~~~~~~~~

The Life and Character of the Late Reverend, Learned, and Pious Mr. Jonathan Edwards was the first book dealing with the life of Edwards. The uniqueness of this volume is as follows: it was produced at the request of Mrs. Jonathan Edwards; it was edited, collected and written by Samuel Hopkins, who was Edwards' literary executor; it was the only biography written by an eyewitness; it was the work of one of Edwards' most gifted students; and it was the labor of one who knew Edwards better than anyone outside of his family. Hopkins in his formative years lived in Edwards' home and studied theology under his direct tutelage. This plus a life time of friendship made Samuel Hopkins the ideal penman for such a task.

All serious students of the life of Edwards have availed themselves of this unique volume. Also, all good biographers of Edwards have been indebted to the Hopkins volume. The volume proffers material collected and written by one who knew Edwards in such a way as to glimpse his heart.

Who was Samuel Hopkins?

Hopkins was born in Waterbury, Connecticut on September 17, 1721 to a farmer. His agrarian father set him apart for the ministry long before the Lord regenerated and called him. He was a descendant of Governor Edward Hopkins of Connecticut.* His college education was at Yale, he entered in September of 1737, and he graduated in 1741. Before finishing at Yale he had in mind to study theology under Gilbert Tennent. However, Hopkins heard Edwards preach in New Haven. He was profoundly impacted and believed he needed to study under him.

Hopkins had not met Edwards but showed up at the parsonage in Northampton, Massachusetts on a winter day in December of 1741 without an invitation. Hopkins had traveled eighty miles from home without notification to or any recommendations to the Edwardses'. Edwards was away on a preaching mission; this was during the time of the Great Awakening. But when he arrived he introduced himself to Sarah Edwards. Mrs. Edwards, who was an extraordinary lady, would have a great impact on his life. "She knew the heart of a stranger" he recounted.

When Jonathan Edwards returned he found he had a new theological student. The two men's lives bonded into a lifelong friendship. Hopkins' life would not be the same after coming under Edwards' roof, for here he came to know Christ as Lord and Saviour; here he also was introduced to Edwardian Calvinism, which would be reflected in his preaching and writing the rest of his life. Being in the Edwards home exposed to the model of a godly home life, attending Edwards preaching was a spiritual boon to his soul, being taught by Edwards opened God's

---

* Edward Hopkins (1600-1657) was born in Shrewsbury, England. He immigrated to the American Colonies in 1637 and settled at Hartford, Connecticut, and was governor of the colony in 1640, 1644, 1646, 1650, 1652 and 1654.

8

eternal and infallible Word, and preaching for Edwards was a remarkable experience for the young man.

Hopkins' observations of Jonathan Edwards and his family have been recorded for posterity by the one who experienced it. He remained with the Edwardses' until late March of 1742 when he returned to his home church to be licensed to preach. He again returned to Northampton in May.

After studying divinity with Jonathan Edwards and having been licensed to preach Hopkins was ordained as pastor of the infant North Parish Church of Housatonick with five members; this was later called Great Barrington, Massachusetts. This settlement, at the time of his arrival, had some thirty families, but Hopkins labored in the ministry there faithfully until 1769. While pastoring there he was instrumental in Edwards' call to Stockbridge after his dismissal from Northampton.

In time Hopkins inadvertently gave offense to his people because of an unusual practice of reading portions of Scripture in the services on the Lord's Day. This was an unusual practice for that era. His faithfulness to this congregation in spite of difficulties was exemplary. There was another kind of danger to face during the French and Indian war for he often had to remove his family to safety.

This church prospered during his pastorate. It went from five to over a hundred during some twenty-five years of his ministry there. His ministry extended beyond the local church he pastored, for he preached to Indians and spent time with Edwards at Stockbridge. He was a patriot and anti-British, he was a high Calvinist and he was strict regarding communion. He became unpopular to the church of which he was used of God to gather there and some stopped supporting the church and some were very poor.

Hopkins' pastorate there came to an end as a result of opposition to his views. However, the pretext for his dismissal was insufficient funds to maintain him. Hopkins was a brilliant man only exceeded by his mentor Jonathan

Edwards. He had been faithful to truth as God had given him the light to understand it and minister it. In great poverty he moved from this place in 1769.

Hopkins was called to the First Church in Newport, Rhode Island. He remained at work in this vineyard from April 1770 until his death on December 20, 1803. When in his first year at Newport George Whitefield visited and ministered to his people. The congregation flourished until the First War for Independence. The town was captured in 1776 by the British and remained under their control for three years. Hopkins remained until he was forced out by the circumstances. During the era of his pastorate being occupied by British soldiers he assisted his friend Dr. Samuel Spring at Newburyport, Mass. He also supplied destitute churches at Canterbury and Stamford, Conn. His congregation at Newport was scattered during occupation and the meeting house virtually destroyed by British soldiers. Upon his return in 1779 he began to preach in a private room, but soon aid from friends in other towns led to the restoration of the meeting place. Although offered other places of ministry he would not leave the beleaguered flock.

Hopkins was a pastor, a reformer and a theologian. His ministry became impaired when he was smitten with paralysis. He was seventy-eight, but continued to preach for four more years. When his ministry began at Newport there was a revival and as his ministry ended there was another revival sent by the Lord. During those days he would pray for each individual church member whom he had on a prayer list. There were thirty-one who professed Christ during the last ingathering. He preached on October 16, 1803 and exclaimed, "Now I have done; I can preach no more." His departure from the pulpit was staggered and he went home to his bed and did not leave until he entered eternity on December 20, 1803.

Williston Walker wrote of Samuel Hopkins,

Personally he was remarkable for force and energy of character, and for the utter fearlessness with which he followed premises to their conclusions. In vigor of intellect and in strength and purity of moral tone he was hardly inferior to Edwards himself.... His training school for negro missionaries to Africa was broken up by the confusion of the American War of Independence.

This servant of the Lord with a ministry beyond the local church he pastored had been recalled by the captain of his salvation.

What is Hopkinsianism?

Hopkins' theological teachings and writings, like those of his teacher Jonathan Edwards, had a powerful influence on New England and perhaps beyond, while his teacher's impact continues to this very hour.

Samuel Hopkins believed that God ruled the universe in such a way as to produce its highest happiness, considered as an entirety; God's sovereignty being absolute therefore sin of necessity must be by divine permission, a means by which this happiness of the whole is secured, but this consequence rendered it heinous in the sinner. Virtue existed for the good of the whole therefore man must willingly accept any disposition that God desires—a doctrine sometimes called "willingness to be damned." He believed all men have the natural power to choose the right, but lack an inclination to choose the right unless God transform him. Thus he believed that preaching must demand an instant submission to God.

What follows is an outline of the basic tenets of Hopkinsianism. The synopsis recorded below is found in *A Theological Dictionary* by Charles Buck. The following also gives a few of the reasons that are brought forward in support of this view.

11

I. That all true virtue or real holiness consists in disinterested benevolence. The object of benevolence is universal being, including God and all intelligent creatures. It wishes and seeks the good of every individual, so far as is consistent with the greatest good for the whole, which is comprised in the glory of God and the perfection and happiness of his kingdom. The law of God is the standard of all moral rectitude or holiness. This is reduced into love to God, and our neighbor as ourselves; and universal good-will comprehends all the love to God, our neighbor and ourselves, required in the divine law, and therefore must be the whole of holy obedience. Let any serious person think what are the particular branches of true piety; when he has viewed each one by itself, he will find that disinterested friendly affections, is its distinguishing characteristic. For instance, all the holiness in pious fear, which distinguishes it from the fear of the wicked, consists in love. Again; holy gratitude is nothing but good-will to God and our neighbor, in which we ourselves are included; and correspondent affection, excited by a view of the good-will and kindness of God. Universal good-will also implies the whole of the duty we owe to our neighbor, for justice, truth, and faithfulness, are comprised in universal benevolence; so are temperance and chastity. For an undue indulgence of our appetites and passions is contrary to benevolence, as tending to hurt ourselves or others; and so opposite to the general good, and the divine command, in which all the crime of such indulgence consists. In short, all virtue is nothing but benevolence acted out in its proper nature and perfection; or love to God and our neighbor, made perfect in all its genuine exercises and expressions.

II. That all sin consists in selfishness. By this is meant an interested, selfish affection by which a person sets himself up as supreme, and the only object of regard; and nothing is good or lovely in his view, unless suited to promote his own private interest. This self-love is in its whole nature, and every degree of it, enmity against God: it is not subject to the law of God, and is the only affection that can oppose it. It is the foundation of all spiritual blindness, and therefore the source of all the open idolatry in the heathen world, and false religion under the light of the Gospel; all this is agreeable to that self-love which opposes God's true character. Under the influence of this principle, men depart from truth; it being itself the greatest practical lie in nature, as it sets up that which is comparatively nothing above universal existence. Self-love is the source of all profaneness and impiety in the world, and of all pride and ambition among men, which is nothing but selfishness acted out in this particular way. This is the foundation of all covetousness and sensuality, as it blinds people's eyes, contracts their hearts, and sinks them down, so that they look upon earthly enjoyments as the greatest good. This is the source of all falsehood, injustice, and oppression, as it excites mankind by undue methods to invade the property of others. Self-love produces all the violent passions; envy, wrath, clamor, and evil speaking: and every thing contrary to the divine law is briefly comprehended in this fruitful source of all iniquity, self-love.

III. That there are no promises of regenerating grace made to the doings of the unregenerate. For as far as men act from self-love, they act from a bad end: for those who have no true love to God, really do no duty when they attend on the externals of religion. And as the unregenerate act from a selfish principle, they do nothing which is commanded: their impenitent doings are wholly opposed to repentance and conversion; therefore not implied in the command to repent, etc.; so far from this, they are altogether disobedient to the command. Hence it appears that there are no promises of salvation to the doings of the unregenerate.

IV. That the impotency of sinners, with respect to believing in Christ, is not natural, but moral; for it is a plain dictate of common sense, that natural impossibility excludes all blame. But an unwilling mind is universally considered as a crime, and not as an excuse, and is the very thing wherein our wickedness consists. That the impotence of the sinner is owing to a disaffection of heart, is evident from the promises of the Gospel. When any object of good is proposed and promised to us upon asking, it clearly evinces that there can be no impotence in us with respect to obtaining it, besides the disapprobation of the will: and that inability which consists in disinclination, never renders any thing improperly the subject of precept or command.

V. That, in order to faith in Christ, a sinner must approve in his heart of the divine conduct, even though God should cast him off for ever; which, however, neither implies love of misery, nor hatred of happiness. For if the law is good, death is due to those who have broken it. The Judge of all the earth cannot but do right. It would bring everlasting reproach upon his government to spare us, considered merely as in ourselves. When this is felt in our hearts, and not till then, we shall be prepared to look to the free grace of God, through the redemption which is in Christ, and to exercise faith in his blood, who is set forth to be a propitiation to declare God's righteousness, that he might be just, and yet be the justifier of him who believeth in Jesus.

VI. That the infinitely wise and holy God has exerted his omnipotent power in such a manner as he purposed should be followed with the existence and entrance of moral evil into the system.—For it must be admitted on all hands, that God has a perfect knowledge, foresight, and view of all possible existences and events. If that system and scene of operation, in which moral evil should never have existed, was actually preferred in the divine mind, certainly the Deity is infinitely disappointed in the issue of his own operations. Nothing can be more dishonorable to God than to imagine that the system which is actually formed by the divine hand, and which was made for his pleasure and glory, is yet not the fruit of wise contrivance and design.

VII. That the introduction of sin is upon the whole, for the general good. For the wisdom and power of the Deity are

14

displayed in carrying on designs of the greatest good; and the existence of moral evil has undoubtedly occasioned a more full, perfect, and glorious discovery of the infinite perfections of the divine nature, than could otherwise have been made to the view of creatures. If the extensive manifestations of the pure and holy nature of God, and his infinite aversion to sin, and all his inherent perfections, in their genuine fruits and effects, is either itself the greatest good or necessarily contains it, it must necessarily follow that the introduction of sin is for the greatest good.

VIII. That repentance is before faith in Christ.—By this is not intended that repentance is before a speculative belief of the being and perfections of God, and of the person and character of Christ; but only that true repentance is previous to a saving faith in Christ, in which the believer is united to Christ, and entitled to the benefits of his mediation and atonement. That repentance is before faith in this sense, appears from several considerations. 1. As repentance and faith respect different objects, so they are distinct exercises of the heart; and therefore one not only may, but must be prior to the other. 2. There may be genuine repentance of sin without faith in Christ, but there cannot be true faith in Christ without repentance of sin; and since repentance is necessary in order to faith in Christ, it must necessarily be prior to faith in Christ. 3. John the Baptist, Christ and his apostles, taught that repentance is before faith. John cried, Repent, for the kingdom of heaven is at hand; intimating that true repentance was necessary in order to embrace the Gospel of the kingdom. Christ commanded, Repent ye, and believe the Gospel. And Paul preached repentance toward God, and faith toward our Lord Jesus Christ.

IX. That though men became sinners by Adam, according to a divine constitution, yet they have and are accountable for no sins but personal; for, 1. Adam's act, in eating the forbidden fruit, was not the act of his posterity; therefore they did not sin at the same time he did. 2. The sinfulness of that act could not be transferred to them afterwards, because the sinfulness of an act can no more be transferred from one person to another than an act itself. 3. Therefore Adam's act, in eating the forbidden fruit, was not the cause, but only the occasion of his posterity's being sinners. God was pleased to make a constitution, that, if Adam remained holy through his state of trial, his posterity should in consequence be holy also; but if he sinned, his posterity should in consequence be sinners likewise. Adam sinned, and now God brings his posterity into the world sinners. By Adam's sin we are become sinners, not for it; his sin being only the occasion, not the cause of our committing sins.

X. That though believers are justified through Christ's righteousness; yet his righteousness is not transferred to them. For, 1. Personal righteousness can no more be transferred from one person to another, than personal sin. 2. If Christ's personal righteousness were transferred to believers, they would be as perfectly holy as Christ; and so stand in no need of forgiveness. 3. But believers are not conscious of having Christ's personal righteousness, but feel and bewail much indwelling sin and corruption. 4. The Scripture represents believers as receiving only the benefits of Christ's righteousness in justification, or their being pardoned and accepted for Christ's righteousness' sake: and this is the proper Scripture notion of imputation. Jonathan's righteousness was imputed to Mephibosheth when David showed kindness to him for his father Jonathan's sake.

The Hopkinsians warmly contend for the doctrine of the divine decrees, that of particular election, total depravity, the special influences of the Spirit of God in regeneration, justification by faith alone, the final perseverance of the saints, and the consistency between entire freedom and absolute dependence; and therefore claim it as their just due, since the world will make distinctions, to be called Hopkinsian Calvinists.

Conclusion

Many biographers have greatly bemoaned the fact that Hopkins did not write a more extended life of Edwards. He had such an understanding of the man, his family and his ministry. Our desire for personal knowledge is commendable, but the providence of God is unchangeable.

The great matter for which all should be thankful is that Samuel Hopkins produced *The Life and Character of the Late Reverend, Learned, and Pious Mr. Jonathan Edwards*. Now Sprinkle Publications brings to the public a new edition of this great work that is foundational to any study of Edwards. There are two items added that were not in the original publication: Edwards' letter to Joseph Hawley and the most famous sermon in the English language *Sinners in the Hands of an Angry God*. This edition is footnoted and a foreword is added.

H. Rondel Rumburg
2008

Bibliography

Carse, James. *Jonathan Edwards & the Visibility of God*. New York: Charles Scribner's Sons. 1967.

Edwards, B. B. and Park, E. A. *Bibliotheca Sacra and Theological Review*, Vol. 1. New York: Wiley and Putnam. 1844.

Edwards, Jonathan, *The Works of*, Vol. I & II. London: Ball, Arnold, and Co., 1840.

Foster, Frank Hugh. *A Genetic History of the New England Theology*. New York: Russell & Russell, Inc. 1963

Gerstner, John H. *The Rational Biblical Theology of Jonathan Edwards*, Vol. I-III. Powhatan: Berea Publications, 1993.

Hagenback, K. R. *A Text-Book of the History of Doctrines*, Vol. II. New York: Sheldon & Co., 1862.

Johnson, Thomas H. *The Printed Writings of Jonathan Edwards: 1703-1758*. New York: Burt Franklin. 1970.

M'Clintock, John and Strong, James. *Cyclopædia of Biblical, Theological, and Ecclesiastical Literature*, Vol. IV. New York: Harper & Brothers, Publishers, 1890.

McGiffert, Arthur Cushman. *Jonathan Edwards*. New York: Harper & Brothers Publishers. 1932.

Miller, Perry. *Jonathan Edwards*. Cleveland: Meridian Books. 1963.

Murray, Iain H. *Jonathan Edwards*. Edinburgh: The Banner of Truth Trust. 1987.

Shedd, William G. T. *A History of Christian Doctrine*, Vol. I-II. Minneapolis: Klock & Klock Christian Publishers. 1978.

Simonson, Harold P. *Jonathan Edwards: Theologian of the Heart*. Grand Rapids: William B. Eerdmans Publishing Company. 1974.

Tracy, Patricia J. *Jonathan Edwards, Pastor: Religion and Society in Eighteenth—Century Northampton*. New York: Hill and Wang. 1980

Turnbull, Ralph G. *Jonathan Edwards the Preacher*. Grand Rapids: Baker Book House. 1958.

Winslow, Ola Elizabeth. *Jonathan Edwards: 1703-1758*. New York: Collier Books. 1961.

CONTENTS

PART I

Containing the history of Edwards' life from birth to his settlement in the work of the ministry.

PART II

Containing extracts from Edwards' private writings, etc.

PART III

Containing a history of Edwards' life from his entering on the work of the ministry to his death.

PART IV

Containing an account of his manuscripts and the books
published by him.

APPENDIX

The Life and Character of Mr. Jonathan Edwards

THE

L I F E

OF THE REVEREND

MR. JONATHAN EDWARDS

~~~~~~~~

PART I

Containing the History of his Life from Birth to his
Settlement in the Work of the Ministry.

$\mathcal{M}$R. JONATHAN EDWARDS was born October 5,
1703, at Windsor, a town in Connecticut. His father was the
Reverend Mr. Timothy Edwards, minister of the gospel on
the east of Connecticut River in Windsor. He began to
reside and preach at Windsor in November 1694, but was
not ordained till July 1698. He died January 27, 1758, in
the 89th year of his age, not two months before this his son.
He was in the work of the ministry above 59 years; and
from his first beginning to reside and preach there, to his
death is above 63 years; and was able to attend on the work
of the ministry and preach constantly till within a few years
before his death. He was very universally esteemed and
beloved as an upright, pious, exemplary man and faithful
minister of the gospel; and was greatly useful. He was born
at Hartford in Connecticut May 14, 1669, received the
honors of the College at Cambridge in New England, by
having the degrees of Bachelor and Master of Arts given
him the same day, July 4, 1694, one in the forenoon, and the
other in the afternoon.

On the 6th day of November 1694 he was married to
Mrs. Esther Stoddard, in the 23rd year of her age, the

daughter of the late famous Mr. Solomon Stoddard* of Northampton; whose great parts and zeal for experimental religion are well known in all the churches in America; and will probably be transmitted to posterity yet unborn, by his valuable writings. They lived together in the married state above 63 years. Mrs. Edwards was born June 2, 1672, and is now living in her 89th year, remarkable for the little decay of her mental powers at so great an age.

---

* Solomon Stoddard was a Congregational pastor. He was born in 1643 at Boston, Massachusetts. Harvard College was his *alma mater*, and he graduated from that institution in 1662. His early labors were as a fellow and first librarian of Harvard. Due to health problems he became chaplain to governor Serle in Barbados, and during his labors there he preached to the Dissenters for almost two years. After his return to the colonies he began to preach at Northampton in 1669. The congregation at Northampton called him to become their pastor March 4th 1670 and he was constituted their minister on September 11, 1672. This was the place where he ministered the rest of his life, and then it pleased the Lord to remove him via death February 11, 1729 (a 57 year pastorate from 1672-1729). Stoddard was responsible for the formulation of the Half-Way Covenant, and issued his apologetical treatise in 1700. This was his first major writing, and was titled *Doctrine of Instituted Churches Explained and Proved from the Word of God*. Stoddard seemed to be in his element arguing theology, and his primary opponent was Increase Mather. As a preacher his messages were clear, pointed, experimental and suggestive. He had five distinct harvests during his ministry, according to his own account, when the Lord awakened many; these, he said, cried out, "What must I do to be saved?" He was a serious student and writer of a number of theological works. *A Guide to Christ* (perhaps his greatest work), *The Safety of appearing on the Day of Judgment in the Righteousness of Christ, Answers to Cases of Conscience* and many other epistles came from his pen. In 1727 Stoddard's grandson Jonathan Edwards became his colleague and successor, but took exception to the Half-Way Covenant. HRR

24

They had eleven children; all which lived to adult years, viz. ten daughters, seven of whom are now living, and this their only son and fifth child.[§]

[§] *As the following more large and particular account of Mr. Edwards' ancestors may gratify some readers, it is inserted here.*

Mr. Edwards' grandfather was Mr. Richard Edwards. His first wife was Mrs. Elisabeth Tuttle, daughter of Mr. William Tuttle of New Haven in Connecticut, and Mrs. Elisabeth Tutle his wife, who came out of Northamptonshire in England. His second wife was Mrs. Talcot, sister to Governor Talcot: by his first wife he had seven children, the oldest of whom was the Reverend Mr. Timothy Edwards of Windsor, his father, before mentioned. By his second wife, Mrs. Talcot, he had six children.

The father of Mr. Richard Edwards was Mr. William Edwards, who came from England young and unmarried. His wife, Mrs. Agnes Edwards, who also came out of England, had two brothers in England, one of them mayor of Exeter, and the other of Barnstable. Mr. William Edwards' father was the Reverend Mr. Richard Edwards, minister of the gospel in London. He lived in Queen Elisabeth's day, and his wife, Mrs. Anne Edwards, assisted in making a ruff (a piece of linen worn around the neck) for the Queen. After the death of Mr. Edwards she married to one Mr. James Cole. She, with her second husband and her son William Edwards, came into America, and all died at Hartford in Connecticut.

Mr. Edwards' grandfather (Mr. Solomon Stoddard and his predecessor at Northampton) married Mrs. Mather, the relict (a widow) of the Reverend Mr. Mather his predecessor, and the first minister at Northamption. Her maiden name was Esther Warham, daughter and youngest child of the Reverend Mr. John Warham, minister at Windsor in Connecticut, who came out of England, before which he was minister in Exerter in England; he had four children, all daughters; and Mrs. Warham survived him, and had two daughters by Mr. Newbury, her second husband.

Mrs. Esther Warham had three children by Mr. Mather, viz. Eunice, Warham and Eliakim. And she had twelve children by Mr. Stoddard, six sons and six dauthers: three of the sons died in infancy. The three that lived to adult years were Anthony, John and Israel. Israel died in prison in France. Anthony was the Reverend Mr. Anthony Stoddard, late minister of the gospel at

Mr. Edwards entered Yale College in the year 1716, and received the degree of Bachelor of Arts in September 1720, a little before he was seventeen years old. He had the character of a sober youth, and a good scholar while he was a member of the college. In his second year at college, and thirteenth of his age, he read (John) Locke on *The Human Understanding* with great delight and profit. His uncommon genius, by which he was as it were by nature formed for closeness of thought and deep penetration, now began to exercise and discover itself. Taking that book into his hand, upon some occasion not long before his death, he said to some of his select friends, who were then with him, that he was beyond expression entertained and pleased with it, when he read it in his youth at college; that he was as much engaged, and had more satisfaction and pleasure in studying

---

Woodbury in Connecticut, who lived to a great age, and was in the work of the ministry sixty years: he died September 6, 1760, in the eighty-second year of his age. John was the Honorable John Stoddard, Esq. who lived at Northampton, and who often, especially in his younger years, served the town as their representative at the great and general court in Boston; and was long head of the county of Hampshire as their chief colonel, and chief judge of the court of common pleas; and he long served his Majesty, and the province of the Massachusetts Bay, as one of his Majesty's council. He was remarkable as a politician, and for his spirit of government: a wise counselor, an upright and skillful judge, a steady and great friend to the interest of religion. He was a great friend and admirer of Mr. Edwards, and greatly strengthened his hands in the work of the ministry while he lived. A more particular account of the life and character of this truly great man may be seen in the sermon which Mr. Edwards preached and published on the occasion of his death.

Mr. Stoddard's father was Anthony Stoddard, Esq. of Boston, a zealous congregational man. He had five wives, the first of which, Mr. Stoddard's mother, was Mrs. Mary Downing, sister to Sir George Downing, whose other sister married Governor Bradstreet. Mr. Solomon Stoddard was their oldest child.

it, than the most greedy miser in gathering up handfuls of silver and gold from some new discovered treasure.

Though he made good proficiency in all the arts and sciences, and had an uncommon taste for natural philosophy, which he cultivated to the end of his life, with that justness and accuracy of thought which was almost peculiar to him; yet Moral Philosophy or Divinity was his favorite study. In this he early made great progress.

He lived at college near two years after he took his first degree, designing and preparing for the work of the ministry. After which, having passed the prerequisite trials, he was licensed to preach the gospel as a candidate. And being pitched upon, and applied to by a number of ministers in New England, who were entrusted to act in behalf of the English Presbyterians at New York, as a fit person to be sent to them, he complied with their request, and went to New York the beginning of August 1722, and preached there to very good acceptance about eight months. But by reason of the smallness of that society, and some special difficulties that attended it, he did not think they were in a capacity to settle a minister, with a rational prospect of answering the good ends proposed. He therefore left them, the next spring and retired to his father's house; where he spent the summer in close study. He was indeed earnestly solicited by the people he had been among at New York, to return to them again; but for the reason just mentioned, he could not think himself in the way of his duty to gratify them.

In September 1723 he received his degree of Master of Arts; about which time he had invitations from several congregations to come among them in order to his settlement in the work of the ministry; but being chosen tutor of Yale College the next spring, in the year 1724, being in the twenty-first year of his age, he retired to the college, and attended the business of tutor there above two years.

While he was in this place he was applied to by the people at Northampton with an invitation to come and settle in the work of the ministry there, with his grandfather Stoddard, who by reason of his great age stood in need of assistance. He therefore resigned his tutorship in September 1726, and accepted of their invitation; and was ordained in the work of the ministry at Northampton, colleague with his grandfather Stoddard, February 15, 1727 in the twenty-fourth year of his age, where he continued in the work of the ministry till June 22, 1750, twenty-three years and four months.

Between the time of his going to New York and his settlement at Northampton he formed a number of resolutions, and committed them to writing; the particular time and special occasion of his making many of them, he has noted in his Diary which he then kept; as well as many other observations and rules, which related to his own exercises and conduct. And as these resolutions, together with the things noted in his Diary, may justly be considered as the foundation and plan of his whole life, it may be proper here to give the reader a taste and idea of them, which will therefore be done in the following extracts.

~~~~~~~~
========

Part II
Containing Extracts from his Private Writings, &c.

***

Section I

HIS RESOLUTIONS

ℬEING sensible that I am unable to do anything without God's help, I do humbly entreat him by his grace to enable me to keep these *Resolutions*, so far as they are agreeable to his will, for Christ's sake.

Remember to Read over these Resolutions *once a week.*

1. Resolved, that I will do whatsoever I think to be most to God's glory, and my own good, profit and pleasure, in the whole of my duration, without any consideration of the time, whether now, or never so many myriads of ages hence. Resolved to do whatever I think to be my duty, and most for the good and advantage of mankind in general. Resolved to do this, whatever difficulties I meet with, how many and how great soever.

2. Resolved, to be continually endeavoring to find out some new invention and contrivance to promote the fore mentioned things.*

---

* The editor is adding in the footnotes the material deleted in the original. HRR 3. Resolved, if ever I shall fall and grow dull, so as to neglect to keep any part of these Resolutions, to repent of all I can remember, when I come to myself again.

4. Resolved, never to do any manner of thing, whether in soul or body, less or more, but what tends to the glory of God; nor be, nor suffer it, if I can avoid it.

5. Resolved, never to loose one moment of time; but improve it the most profitable way I possibly can.

6. Resolved, to live with all my might, while I do live.

7. Resolved, never to do anything, which I should be afraid to do, if it were the last hour of my life.[§]

9. Resolved, to think much on all occasions of my own dying, and of the common circumstances which attend death.[+]

11. Resolved, when I think of any theorem in divinity to be solved, immediately to do what I can towards solving it, if circumstances do not hinder.[×]

13. Resolved, to be endeavoring to find out fit objects of charity and liberality.

14. Resolved, never to do anything out of revenge.

15. Resolved, never to suffer the least motions of anger to irrational beings.[*]

17. Resolved, that I will live so as I shall wish I had done when I come to die.

[§] 8. Resolved, to act, in all respects, both speaking and doing, as if nobody had been so vile as I, and as if I had committed the same sins, or had the same infirmities or failings as others; and that I will let the knowledge of their failings promote nothing but shame in myself, and prove only an occasion of my confessing my own sins and misery to God.

[+] 10. Resolved, when I feel pain, to think of the pains of martyrdom, and of hell.

[×] 12. Resolved, if I take delight in it as a gratification of pride, or vanity, or on any such account, immediately to throw it by.

[*] 16. Resolved, never to speak evil of anyone, so that it shall tend to his dishonor, more or less, upon no account except for some real good.

18. Resolved, to live so at all times, as I think is best in my devout frames, and when I have clearest notions of things of the gospel, and another world.[§]

20. Resolved, to maintain the strictest temperance in eating and drinking.

21. Resolved, never to do anything, which if I should see in another, I should count a just occasion to despise him for, or to think any way the more meanly of him.[+]

24. Resolved, whenever I do any conspicuously evil action, to trace it back, till I come to the original cause; and then both carefully endeavor to do so no more, and to fight and pray with all my might against the original of it.[×]

28. Resolved, to study the Scriptures so steadily, constantly and frequently, as that I may find, and plainly perceive myself to grow in the knowledge of the same.[*]

[§] 19. Resolved, never to do anything, which I should be afraid to do, if I expected it would not be above an hour, before I should hear the last trump.

[+] 22. Resolved, to endeavor to obtain for myself as much happiness, in the other world, as I possibly can, with all the power, might, vigor, and vehemence, yea violence, I am capable of, or can bring myself to exert, in any way that can be thought of.

23. Resolved, frequently to take some deliberate action, which seems most unlikely to be done, for the glory of God, and trace it back to the original intention, designs and ends of it; and if I find it not to be for God's glory, to repute it as a breach of the 4th Resolution.

[×] 25. Resolved, to examine carefully, and constantly, what that one thing in me is, which causes me in the least to doubt of the love of God; and to direct all my forces against it.

26. Resolved, to cast away such things, as I find do abate my assurance.

27. Resolved, never willfully to omit anything, except the omission be for the glory of God; and frequently to examine my omissions.

[*] 29. Resolved, never to count that a prayer, nor to let that pass as a prayer, nor that as a petition of a prayer, which is so made, that I

30. Resolved, to strive to my utmost every week to be brought higher in religion, and to a higher exercise of grace, than I was the week before.[§]

32. Resolved, to be strictly and firmly faithful to my trust, that that in Prov. 20:6, *"A faithful man who can find?"* may not be partly fulfilled in me.

33. Resolved, always to do what I can towards making, maintaining, establishing and preserving peace, when it can be without over balancing detriment in other respects.

34. Resolved, in narrations never to speak anything but the pure and simple verity.[+]

36. Resolved, never to speak evil of any, except I have some particular good call for it.

37. Resolved, to inquire every night, as I am going to bed, wherein I have been negligent, what sin I have committed, and wherein I have denied myself: also at the end of every week, month and year.

38. Resolved, never to speak anything that is ridiculous, sportive, or matter of laughter on the Lord's Day.

39. Resolved, never to do anything that I so much question the lawfulness of, as that I intend, at the same time, to consider and examine afterwards, whether it be lawful or

---

cannot hope that God will answer it; nor that as a confession, which I cannot hope God will accept.

[§] 31. Resolved, never to say anything at all against anybody, but when it is perfectly agreeable to the highest degree of Christian honor, and of love to mankind, agreeable to the lowest humility, and sense of my own faults and failings, and agreeable to the golden rule; often, when I have said anything against anyone, to bring it to, and try it strictly by the test of this Resolution.

[+] 35. Resolved, whenever I so much question whether I have done my duty, as that my quiet and calm is thereby disturbed, to set it down, and also how the question was resolved.

no: except I as much question the lawfulness of the omission.[x]

41. Resolved, to ask myself at the end of every day, week, month and year, wherein I could possibly in any respect have done better.

42. Resolved, frequently to renew the dedication of myself to God, which was made at my baptism; which I solemnly renewed, when I was received into the communion of the church; and which I have solemnly remade this twelfth day of January, 1722-23.

43. Resolved, never henceforward, till I die, to act as if I were any way my own, but entirely and altogether God's, agreeable to what is to be found in Saturday, January 12.[*]

46. Resolved, never to allow the least measure of any fretting uneasiness at my father or mother. Resolved to suffer no effects of it, so much as in the least alteration of speech, or motion of my eye: and to be especially careful of it, with respect to any of our family.

47. Resolved, to endeavor to my utmost to deny whatever is not most agreeable to a good, and universally sweet and benevolent, quiet, peaceable, contented, easy, compassionate, generous, humble, meek, modest, submissive, obliging, diligent and industrious, charitable, even, patient, moderate, forgiving, sincere temper; and to do at all times what such a temper would lead me to: examine strictly every week, whether I have done so.

---

[x] 40. Resolved, to inquire every night, before I go to bed, whether I have acted in the best way I possibly could, with respect to eating and drinking.

[*] 44. Resolved, that no other end but religion, shall have any influence at all on any of my actions; and that no action shall be, in the least circumstance, any otherwise than the religious end will carry it.

45. Resolved, never to allow any pleasure or grief, joy or sorrow, nor any affection at all, nor any degree of affection, nor any circumstance relating to it, but what helps religion.

48. Resolved, constantly, with the utmost niceness and diligence, and the strictest scrutiny, to be looking into the state of my soul, that I may know whether I have truly an interest in Christ or no; that when I come to die, I may not have any negligence respecting this to repent of.[§]

50. Resolved, I will act so as I think I shall judge would have been best, and most prudent, when I come into the future world.[+]

52. I frequently hear persons in old age say how they would live, if they were to live their lives over again: Resolved, that I will live just so as I can think I shall wish I had done, supposing I live to old age.[x]

54. Whenever I hear anything spoken in conversation of any person, if I think it would be praiseworthy in me, Resolved to endeavor to imitate it.

55. Resolved, to endeavor to my utmost to act as I can think I should do, if I had already seen the happiness of heaven, and hell torments.

56. Resolved, never to give over, nor in the least to slacken my fight with my corruptions, however unsuccessful I may be.

57. Resolved, when I fear misfortunes and adversities, to examine whether I have done my duty, and resolve to do it; and let it be just as providence orders it, I will as far as I can, be concerned about nothing but my duty and my sin.[*]

[§] 49. Resolved, that this never shall be, if I can help it.

[+] 51. Resolved, that I will act so, in every respect, as I think I shall wish I had done, if I should at last be damned.

[x] 53. Resolved, to improve every opportunity, when I am in the best and happiest frame of mind, to cast and venture my soul on the Lord Jesus Christ, to trust and confide in him, and consecrate myself wholly to him; that from this I may have assurance of my safety, knowing that I confide in my Redeemer.

[*] 58. Resolved, not only to refrain from an air of dislike, fretfulness, and anger in conversation, but to exhibit an air of love, cheerfulness and benignity.

62. Resolved, never to do anything but duty; and then according to Eph. 6:6-8, do it willingly and cheerfully as unto the Lord, and not to man; *"knowing that whatever good thing any man doth, the same shall he receive of the Lord."* §

65. Resolved, very much to exercise myself in this all my life long, viz. with the greatest openness I am capable of, to declare my ways to God, and lay open my soul to him: all my sins, temptations, difficulties, sorrows, fears, hopes, desires, and every thing, and every circumstance;

---

59. Resolved, when I am most conscious of provocations to ill nature and anger, that I will strive most to feel and act good-naturedly; yea, at such times, to manifest good nature, though I think that in other respects it would be disadvantageous, and so as would be imprudent at other times.

60. Resolved, whenever my feelings begin to appear in the least out of order, when I am conscious of the least uneasiness within, or the least irregularity without, I will then subject myself to the strictest examination.

61. Resolved, that I will not give way to that listlessness which I find unbends and relaxes my mind from being fully and fixedly set on religion, whatever excuse I may have for it--that what my listlessness inclines me to do, is best to be done, etc.

§ 63. On the supposition, that there never was to be but one individual in the world, at any one time, who was properly a complete Christian, in all respects of a right stamp, having Christianity always shining in its true luster, and appearing excellent and lovely, from whatever part and under whatever character viewed: Resolved, to act just as I would do, if I strove with all my might to be that one, who should live in my time.

64. Resolved, when I find those *"groanings which cannot be uttered"* (Rom. 8:26), of which the Apostle speaks, and those *"breakings of soul for the longing it hath,"* of which the Psalmist speaks, Psalm 119:20, that I will promote them to the utmost of my power, and that I will not be weary of earnestly endeavoring to vent my desires, nor of the repetitions of such earnestness.

according to Dr. (Thomas) Manton's 27th Sermon on the 119 Psalm.[+]

67. Resolved, after afflictions, to inquire, what I am the better for them, what good I have got by them, and what I might have got by them.[×] [*]

[+] 66. Resolved, that I will endeavor always to keep a benign aspect, and air of acting and speaking in all places, and in all companies, except it should so happen that duty requires otherwise.

[×] 68. Resolved, to confess frankly to myself all that which I find in myself, either infirmity or sin; and, if it be what concerns religion, also to confess the whole case to God, and implore needed help.

69. Resolved, always to do that, which I shall wish I had done when I see others do it.

70. Let there be something of benevolence, in all that I speak.

[*] The *Resolutions* are seventy in number. But part of them are here transcribed, as a specimen of the whole. The number here affixed to them is that by which they are numbered in the original manuscript; and retained here for the sake of the references made to some of them in the Diary, as the reader will presently see. [*The editor of the Sprinkle edition has footnoted the other numbers*]

***

SECTION II

EXTRACTS FROM HIS PRIVATE DIARY

Saturday, Dec. 22, 1722, This day, revived by God's Holy Spirit; affected with the sense of the excellency of holiness; felt more exercise of love to Christ, than usual. Have, also, felt sensible repentance for sin, because it was committed against so merciful and good a God. This night made the 37th Resolution.

Sabbath day night, Dec. 23, 1722. Made the 38th Resolution.

Monday, Dec. 24. Higher thoughts than usual of the excellency of Jesus Christ and his kingdom.

Wednesday, Jan. 2, 1722-3. Dull. I find, by experience, that let me make resolutions, and do what I will, with never so many inventions, it is all nothing, and to no purpose at all, without the motions of the Spirit of God; for if the Spirit of God should be as much withdrawn from me always, as for the week past, notwithstanding all I do, I should not grow, but should languish, and miserably fade away.... There is no dependence on myself. It is to no purpose to resolve, except we depend on the grace of God; for, if it were not for his mere grace, one might be a very good man one day, and a very wicked one the next.

Sabbath day, Jan. 6, at night. Much concerned about the improvement of precious time. Intend to live in continual mortification, without ceasing, and even to weary myself thereby as long as I am in this world.

Tuesday, Jan. 8, in the morning. Had higher thoughts than usual of the excellency of Christ, and felt an unusual repentance of sin therefrom.

Wednesday, Jan. 9, at night. Decayed. I am sometimes apt to think, that I have a great deal more of holiness than I really have. I find now and then that abominable corruption, which is directly contrary to what I read of eminent Christians.... How deceitful is my heart! I take up a strong resolution, but how soon doth it weaken! *Thursday*, Jan. 10, about noon. Reviving. 'Tis a great dishonor to Christ, in whom I hope I have an interest, to be uneasy at my worldly state and condition. When I see the prosperity of others, and that all things go easy with them; the world is smooth to them, and they are happy in many respects, and very prosperous, or are advanced to much honor; to grudge and envy them, or be the least uneasy at it; to wish and long for the same prosperity, and to desire that is should ever be so with me. Wherefore, concluded always to rejoice in every one's prosperity, and that it would ever be so with me. Wherefore concluded always to rejoice in every one's prosperity, and to expect for myself no happiness of that nature as long as I live; but to depend on afflictions, and to betake myself entirely to another happiness.

I think I find myself much more sprightly and healthy, both in body and mind, for my self-denial in eating, drinking, and sleeping.

I think it would be advantageous every morning to consider my business and temptations; and what sins shall be exposed on that day; and to make a resolution how to improve the day, and avoid those sins. And so at the beginning of every week, month, and year.

I never knew before what was meant, by not setting our hearts on those things. 'Tis, not to care about them, to depend upon them, to afflict ourselves with the fears of losing them, nor please ourselves with expectation of obtaining them, or hope of continuance of them. At night made the 41st Resolution.

Saturday, Jan. 12, in the morning. I have this day solemnly renewed my baptismal covenant and self-dedication, which I renewed when I was received into the communion of the church. I have been before God; and have given myself, all that I am and have to God so that I

38

am not in any respect, my own: I can challenge no right in myself, I can challenge no right in this understanding, this will, these affections, which are in me. Neither have I any right to this body, or any of its members; no right to this tongue, these hands, these feet; no right to these senses, these eyes, these ears, this smell, or this taste. I have been to God this morning, and told him, that I gave myself *wholly* to him. I have given every power to him; so that, for the future I will challenge no right in myself, in no respect. I have expressly promised him, and do now promise Almighty God, that by his grace I will not. I have this morning told him, that I did take him for my whole portion and felicity, looking on nothing else as any part of my happiness, nor acting as if it were; and his law for the constant rule of my obedience; and would fight with all my might against the world, the flesh, and the devil, to the end of my life. And did believe in Jesus Christ, and receive him as a Prince and Saviour; and would adhere to the faith and obedience of the gospel, however hazardous and difficult soever the profession and practice of it may be. That I did receive the blessed Spirit as my teacher, sanctifier, and only comforter; and cherish all his motions to enlighten, purify, confirm, comfort and assist me. This, I have done. And I pray God, for the sake of Christ, to look upon it as a self-dedication; and to receive me now as entirely his own, and to deal with me, in all respects as such; whether he afflicts me or prospers me, or whatever he pleases to do with me, who am his. Now, henceforth, I am not to act, in any respect, as my own.—I shall act as my own, if I ever make use of any of my powers to any thing that is not to the glory of God, and do not make the glorifying of him my whole and entire business; if I murmur in the least at afflictions; if I grieve at the prosperity of others; if I am in any way uncharitable; if I am angry because of injuries; if I revenge; if I do any thing purely to please myself, or if I avoid any thing for the sake of my own ease; if I omit any thing because it is great self-denial; if I trust to myself; if I take any of the praise of the good that I do, or rather God does by me; or if I am in any way proud.

This day, made the 42nd and 43rd Resolutions.

Monday, Jan. 14. The dedication I made of myself to God on Saturday last, has been exceedingly useful to me. I thought I had a more spiritual insight into the Scripture, reading the 8th chapter of the Romans, than ever in my life before.

Great instances of mortification are deep wounds given to the body of sin; hard blows that make him stagger and reel: we thereby get strong ground and footing against him.... While we live without great instances of mortification and self-denial, the old man keeps whereabouts he was; for he is sturdy and obstinate, and will not stir for small blows. After the greatest mortifications, I always find the greatest comfort.

Supposing there was never but one complete Christian, in all respects, of a right stamp, having Christianity shining in its true luster, at a time in the world; resolved to act just as I would do, if I strove with all my might to be that one, that should be in my time.

Tuesday, Jan. 15. It seemed yesterday, the day before, and Saturday, that I should always retain the same resolutions to the same height; but alas! how soon do I decay! O how weak, how infirm, how unable to do any thing am I! What a poor, inconsistent what a miserable wretch, without the assistance of God's Spirit! While I stand, I am ready to think that I stand by my own strength, and upon my own legs; and I am ready to triumph over my spiritual enemies, as if it were I myself that caused them to flee: when alas! I am but a poor infant, upheld by Jesus Christ; who holds me up, and gives me liberty to smile to see my enemies flee, when he drives them before me; and so I laugh, as though I myself did it, when it is only Jesus Christ leads me along, and fights himself against my enemies. And now the Lord has a little left me, and how weak do I find myself! O! let it teach me to depend less on myself, to be more humble, and to give more of the praise of my ability to Jesus Christ! The heart of man is deceitful above all things, and desperately wicked; who can know it?

Saturday, Feb. 16. I do certainly know that I love holiness, such as the gospel requires.

At night. I have been negligent for the month past, in these three things: I have not been watchful enough over my appetites, in eating and drinking; in rising too late a-mornings; and in not applying myself with sufficient application to the duty of secret prayer.

Sabbath day, Feb 17, near sunset. Renewedly promised that I will accept of God, for my whole portion; and that I will be contented, whatever else I am denied. I will not murmur, nor be grieved, whatever prosperity upon any account I see others enjoy and I am denied. I will not murmur, nor be grieved, whatever prosperity, upon any account, I see others enjoy, and I am denied.

Saturday, March 2. O how much pleasanter is humility than pride! O that God would fill me with exceeding great humility, and that he would evermore keep me from all pride! The pleasures of humility are really the most refined, inward and exquisite delights in the world. How hateful is a proud man! How hateful is a worm that lifts up itself with pride! What a foolish, silly, miserable, blind, deceived poor worm am I, when pride works.

Wednesday, March 6, near sunset. Felt the doctrines of election, free grace, and of our not being able to do any thing without the grace of God; and that holiness is entirely, throughout, the work of God's Spirit, with more pleasure than before.

Monday morning, April 1*. I think it best not to allow myself to laugh at the faults, follies and infirmities of others.

Saturday night, April 6§. This week I found myself so far gone that it seemed to me that I should never recover

---

* This is April 2nd in other copies. HRR

more. Let God of his mercy return unto me, and no more leave me thus to sink and decay! I know, O Lord, that without thy help I shall fall innumerable times, not withstanding all my resolutions, how often soever repeated.

Saturday night, April 13[x]. I could pray more heartily this night for the forgiveness of my enemies, than ever before.

Wednesday, May 1, forenoon. Last night I came home, after my melancholy parting from New York.

I have always, in every different state of life I have hitherto been in, thought that the troubles and difficulties of that state to be greater than those of any other that I proposed to be in; and when I have altered, with assurance of mending myself, I have still thought the same; yea, that the difficulties of that state are greater than those of that I left last. Lord, grant that from hence I may learn to withdraw thoughts, affections, desires and expectations entirely from the world, and may fix them upon the heavenly state; where there is fullness of joy; where reigns heavenly, sweet, calm and delightful love without alloy; where there are continually the dearest expressions of this love; where there is the enjoyment of the persons loved, without ever parting; and where those persons, who appear so lovely in this world, will really be inexpressibly more lovely, and full of love to us. How sweetly will the mutual lovers join together in singing the praises of God and the Lamb! How full will it fill us with joy to think that this enjoyment, these sweet exercises, will never cease or come to an end, but will last to all eternity.

Remember, after journeys, removals, overturnings and alterations in the state of my life, to reflect and consider, whether therein I have managed the best way possible, respecting my soul? and before such alterations, if foreseen, to resolve how to act.

[§] This is April 7th in other copies. HRR
[x] This is April 14th in other copies. HRR

Thursday, May 2. I think it a very good way, to examine dreams every morning when I awake; what are the nature, circumstance, principles and ends of my imaginary actions and passions in them to discern what are my prevailing inclinations, etc.

Saturday night, May 4. Although I have in some measure, subdued a disposition to chide and fret, yet I find a certain inclination, which is not agreeable to Christian sweetness of temper and conversation: either too much dogmaticalness or too much of the egotism; a disposition to be telling my own dislike and scorn, and my own freedom from those which are innocent, sinless, yea common infirmities of men, and many other such like things. O that God would help me to discern all the flaws and defects of my temper and conversation, and help me in the difficult work of amending them; and that he would fill me so full of Christianity, that the foundation of all those disagreeable irregularities may be destroyed, and the contrary sweetnesses and beauties may of themselves naturally follow.

Sabbath day, May 5 in the morning. This day made the 47th Resolution.

Sabbath day morning, May 12. I think I find in my heart to be glad from the hopes I have, that my eternity is to be spent in spiritual and holy joys, arising from the manifestation of God's love, and the exercise of holiness and burning love to him.

Saturday night, May 18. I now plainly perceive what great obligations I am under to love and honor my parents. I have great reason to believe that their counsel and education have been my making, notwithstanding, in the time of it, it seemed to do me so little good. I have good reason to hope, that their prayers for me have been, in many things, very powerful and prevalent; that God has, in many things, taken me under his care and guidance, provision and direction, in answer to their prayers for me. I was never made so sensible of it as now.

Wednesday, May 22, in the morning. *Memorandum*. To take special care of the following things: evil speaking, fretting, eating, drinking and sleeping, speaking simple verity, joining in prayer, slightness in secret prayer, listlessness and negligence, and thoughts that cherish sin.

Saturday, May 25, in the morning. As I was this morning reading the 17th Resolution, it was suggested to me, that if I were now to die, I should wish that I had prayed more that God would make me know my state, whether it be good or bad; and that I had taken more pains to see and narrowly search into that matter. Wherefore, *Mem*, for the future, most nicely and diligently to look into our old divines opinions concerning conversion. Made the 48th Resolution.

Friday afternoon, June 1*. Afternoon. I have abundant cause, O my merciful Father, to love thee ardently, and greatly to bless and praise thee, that thou hast heard me in my earnest request, and so hast answered my prayer for mercy, to keep from decay and sinking. O, graciously, of thy mere goodness, still continue to pity my misery, by reason of my sinfulness. O, my dear Redeemer, I commit myself, together with my prayer and thanksgiving, into thine hand.

Monday, July 1§. Again confirmed by experience of the happy effects of strict temperance, with respect both to body and mind. Resolved for the future to observe rather more of meekness, moderation and temper in disputes.

Thursday, July 18, near sunset. Resolved, to endeavor to make sure of that sign the Apostle James gives of a perfect man, James 3:2, *"If any man offend not in word, the same is a perfect man, and able, also, to bridle the whole body."*

Monday, July 22. I see there is danger, of my being drawn into transgression by the power of such

---

* Other editions have this as June 21. HRR
§ Part of July 4th in other copies. HRR

temptations as the fear of seeming uncivil, and of offending friends. Watch against it.

Tuesday, July 23. When I find those groanings which cannot be uttered, the Apostle speaks of; and those soul-breakings, for the longing it hath, of which the Psalmist speaks of Psalm 119:20 to humor and promote them, to the utmost of my power, and not to be weary of earnestly endeavoring to vent my desires.

To count it all joy, when I have occasion of great self-denial, because then I have a glorious opportunity of giving deadly wounds to the body of sin, and of greatly confirming and establishing the new nature: to seek to mortify sin, and increase in holiness. These are the best opportunities, according to January 14.

To improve afflictions, of all kinds as blessed opportunities of forcibly bearing on in my Christian course, notwithstanding that which is so very apt to discourage me, and to damp the vigor of my mind, and to make me lifeless; also, as opportunities of trusting and confiding in God, and getting a habit of so doing, according to the 57th Resolution. And as an opportunity of rending my heart off from the world, and setting it on heaven alone. To improve them, also, as opportunities to repent of and bewail my sin, and abhor myself; and as a blessed opportunity to exercise patience; to trust in God, and divest my mind from the affliction, by fixing myself in religious exercises. Also, let me comfort myself that it is the very nature of afflictions to make the heart better; and if I am made better by them, what need I be concerned, however grievous they seem for the present.

Friday afternoon, July 26. To be particularly careful to keep up inviolably, a trust and reliance, ease and entire rest in God, in all conditions, according to the 57th Resolution; for this I have found to be wonderfully advantageous to me.

Monday, July 29. When I am concerned how I shall prepare any thing to public acceptance, to be very careful that I have it very clear to me, that I do what is duty and prudence in the matter.

Wednesday, July 31. Never in the least to seek to hear sarcastical relations of others faults. Never to give credit to any thing said against others, except there is very plain reason for it; nor to behave in any respect the otherwise for it.

Wednesday, Aug. 7. To esteem it as some advantage, that the duties of religion are difficult, and that many difficulties are sometimes to be gone through, in the way of duty. Religion is the sweeter, and what is gained by labor is abundantly more precious, as a woman loves her child the better for having brought it forth with travail. And even to Christ Jesus himself his mediatorial glory, his victory and triumph, the kingdom which he hath obtained, how much more glorious is it, how much more excellent and precious, for his having wrought it out with such agonies!

Friday, Aug. 9. One thing that may be a good help towards thinking profitably in time of vacation is, when I find a profitable thought ,that I can fix my mind on, to follow it as far as I possibly can to advantage.

Sabbath day, Aug. 11, after meeting. Resolved always to do that, which I shall wish I had done when I see others do it. As for instance, sometimes I argue with myself, that such an act of good nature, kindness, forbearance or forgiveness, etc. is not my duty, because it will have such and such consequences: yet when I see others do it, then it appears amiable to me, and I wish I had done it; and see that none of these feared inconveniences follow.

Tuesday, Aug. 13. I find it would be very much to my advantage, to be thoroughly acquainted with the Scriptures. When I am reading doctrinal books, or books of controversy, I can proceed with abundantly more confidence; can see on what footing and foundation I stand.

Thursday, Aug. 29*. The objection my corruptions make against doing whatever my hand finds to do with my might is that it is a constant mortification. Let this objection by no means ever prevail.

Monday, Sept. 2. There is much folly, when I am quite sure I am in the right, and others are positive in contradicting me, to enter into a vehement or long debate upon it.

Monday, Sept. 23. I observe that old men seldom have any advantage of new discoveries; because they are beside the way of thinking, they have been so long used to. Resolved, if ever I live to years, that I will be impartial to hear the reasons of all pretended discoveries, and receive them, if rational, how long soever I have been used to another way of thinking.

Thursday, Oct. 18. To follow the example of Mr. B. who though he meets with great difficulties, yet undertakes them with a smiling countenance, as though he thought them but little; and speaks of them as if they were very small.

Tuesday, Nov. 26. It is a most evil and pernicious practice, in meditations on afflictions, to sit ruminating on the aggravations of the affliction, and reckoning up the evil, dark circumstances thereof, and dwelling long on the dark side; it doubles and trebles the affliction. And so when speaking of them together, to make them as bad as we can, and use our eloquence to set forth our own troubles, and are all the while making new trouble, and feeding and pampering the old; whereas the contrary practice would starve our afflictions. If we dwelt on the light side of things in our thoughts, and

---

* This is recorded under Saturday night August 31 in other accounts. HRR

extenuated them all that possibly we could, when speaking of them, we should think little of them ourselves; and the affliction would really, in a great measure, vanish away.

Thursday night, Dec. 12. If at any time I am forced to tell others wherein I think they are something to blame; for the avoiding the important evil that would otherwise ensue, not to tell it to them; so that there shall be a probability of their taking it as the effect of little fretting, angry emotions of mind.

Tuesday night, Dec. 31. Concluded never to suffer nor express any angry emotions of mind more or less except the honor of God calls for it, in zeal for him, or to preserve myself from being trampled on.

Wednesday, Jan. 1, 1724. Not to spend too much time in thinking, even of important and necessary worldly business. To allow every thing its proportion of thought, according to its urgency and importance.

Friday, Jan. 10, 1723-4. [After having written considerable in short hand, which he used, when he would have what he wrote, effectually concealed from every body but himself, he notes the following words in round hand], remember to act according to Proverbs 12:23, *"A prudent man concealeth knowledge."*

Monday, Feb. 3. Let every thing have the value now, that it will have upon a sick bed: and frequently in my pursuits of whatever kind, let this come into my mind; "How much shall I value this upon my deathbed?"

Wednesday, Feb. 5. Have not in time past, in my prayers, enough insisted upon the glorifying of God in the world, on the advancement of the kingdom of Christ, the prosperity of the church, and the good of men. Determined that this objection is without weight, *viz.* that it is not likely that God will make great alterations in the whole world, and overturnings in kingdoms and nations, only for the prayers of one obscure person, seeing such things used to be done in answer to the united, earnest prayers of the whole church; and that if my prayers should have some influence, it would be but imperceptible and small.

Thursday, Feb. 6. More convinced than ever, of the usefulness of free religious conversation. I find by conversing on natural philosophy, I gain knowledge abundantly faster, and see the reasons of things much clearer than in private study. Wherefore earnestly to seek at all times for religious conversation; for those that I can with profit and delight, and freedom so converse with.

Sabbath day, Feb. 23. If I act according to my resolution, I shall desire riches no otherwise than as they are helpful to religion. But this I determine, as what is really evident from many parts of Scripture, that to fallen man they have a greater tendency to hurt religion.

Saturday, May 23. How it comes about I know not; but I have remarked it hitherto, that at those times when I have read the Scripture most, I have evermore been most lively, and in the best frame.

Saturday night, June 6. This week has been a very remarkable week with me with respect to despondencies, fears, perplexities, multitudes of cares, and distraction of mind; it being the week I came hither to New Haven, in order to entrance upon the office of Tutor of the College. I have now abundant reason to be convinced of the troublesomeness and vexation of the world, and that it will never be another kind of world.

Tuesday, July 7. When I am giving the relation of a thing, to abstain from altering either in the matter or manner of speaking, so much, as that if every one afterward should alter as much, it would at last come to be properly false.

Tuesday, Sept. 2. By a sparingness in diet, and eating, as much as may be, what is light and easy of digestion, I shall doubtless be able to think clearer, and shall gain time; 1st, By lengthening out my life; 2ndly. Shall need less time for digestion, after meals; 3rdly. Shall be able to study more closely, without injury to my health; 4thly. Shall need less time for sleep; 5thly. Shall seldom be troubled with the headache.

Sabbath, Nov. 22. Considering that bystanders always espy some faults which we do not see ourselves, or at least are not so fully sensible of; there are many secret workings of corruption which escape our sight, and of which others only are sensible of: resolved therefore, that I will, if I can by any convenient means, learn what faults others find in me, or what things they see in me, that appear any way blameworthy, unlovely or unbecoming.

***

Section III

REFLECTION ON THE FOREGOING EXTRACTS

The foregoing Extracts were written by Mr. Edwards in the twentieth and twenty-first years of his age, as appears by the dates. This being kept in mind the judicious reader will make proper allowance for some things, which may appear a little juvenile or like a young Christian, as to the matter of manner of expression; which would not have been found; had it not have been done in early life. Which, indeed, are no blemishes, the whole being taken together: as by this it appears more natural, and the strength of his resolution and fervor of mind; and his skill and discerning in divine things, so seldom found even in old age, are the more striking. And in this view we shall be led to admire his conscientious strictness, his zeal and painfulness, his experience and judgment in true religion at so early an age. For here are not only the most convincing evidences of sincerity and thorough religion, of his engaging in a life devoted to God in good earnest, so as to make religion his only business; but through his great attention to this matter, he appears to have the judgment and experience of grey hairs.

This is the beginning of a life so eminently holy and useful as Mr. Edwards' was. He, who became one of the greatest divines in this age, has had the applause and admiration of America, Britain, Holland and Germany for his piety, and great judgment and skill in divinity; and has been honored above most others in the Christian world in this century, in his being made the instrument of doing so much good: he began his life thus; he entered on a public life with such views, such exercises, such resolutions.

This may serve as a direction and excitement to those who are young to devote themselves to God in good earnest, and enter on the business of strict and thorough religion without delay: especially those who are looking towards the work of the ministry, as they would take the most direct, the only way to answer the good ends which they profess to seek.

It is to be lamented that, there is so much reason to think, there are so few instances of such early piety in our day. If the Protestant world abounded with young persons of this stamp: with young men, who were preparing for the work of the ministry, with such a temper, such exercises and such resolutions; what a delightful prospect would this afford of the near approach of happier days than the church of God has ever yet seen! What pleasing hopes that the great, the merciful Head of the church was about to send forth laborers, faithful successful laborers into his harvest; and bless his people with "pastors which shall feed them with knowledge and understanding!"

But if our youth neglect all proper improvement of the mind; are shy of seriousness and strict piety; choose to live strangers to it and keep at a distance from all appearance of it; are wanton and given to carnal pleasures; what a gloomy prospect does this afford! If they, who enter into the work of the ministry, from a gay, careless and what may justly be called a vicious life, betake themselves to a little superficial study of divinity, and soon begin to preach, while all the externals, seriousness and zeal they put on is only from worldly motives, they begin without any inward, experimental acquaintance with spiritual, divine things and even so much as any taste for true divinity, no wonder if the churches "suck dry breasts," and there are many ignorant watchmen.

But, as the best comment on the foregoing Resolutions and Diary, and that the reader may have a more particular, full and instructive view of Mr. Edwards' entrance on a religious life, and progress in it as consisting in the views and exercises of his mind, a brief account thereof is here inserted, which was found among his papers, in his own

52

handwriting; and which, it seems, was written nearly twenty years after for his own private advantage.

***

SECTION IV

AN ACCOUNT OF HIS CONVERSION, EXPERIENCES AND RELIGIOUS EXERCISES GIVEN BY HIMSELF

I had a variety of concerns and exercises about my soul from my childhood; but had two more remarkable seasons of awakening before I met with that change by which I was brought to those new dispositions, and that new sense of things that I have since had. The first time was when I was a boy, some years before I went to college, at a time of remarkable awakening in my father's congregation. I was then very much affected for many moths, and concerned about the things of religion and my soul's salvation; and was abundant in duties. I used to pray five times a day in secret, and to spend much time in religious talk with other boys, and used to meet with them to pray together. I experienced I know not what kind of delight in religion. My mind was much engaged in it, and had much self-righteous pleasure, and it was my delight to abound in religious duties. I, with some of my schoolmates joined together, built a booth in a swamp, in a very secret and retired place, for a place of prayer. And besides, I had particular secret places of my own in the woods, where I used to retire by myself; and used to be from time to time much affected. My affections seemed to be lively and easily moved, and I seemed to be in my element when I engaged in religious duties. And I am ready to think many are deceived with such affections, and such a kind of delight, as I then had in religion, and mistake it for grace.

But, in process of time, my convictions and affections wore off, and I entirely lost all those affections and delights, and left off secret prayer, at least as to any constant performance of it, and returned like a dog to his vomit, and went on in ways of sin.

Indeed I was at sometimes very uneasy, especially towards the latter part of the time of my being at college, till it pleased God, in my last year at college, at a time when I was in the midst of many uneasy thoughts about the state of my soul, to seize me with a pleurisy; in which He brought me nigh to the grave, and shook me over the pit of hell.

But yet it was not long after my recovery before I fell again into my old ways of sin. But God would not suffer me to go on with any quietness, but I had great and violent inward struggles; until after many conflicts with wicked inclinations, and repeated resolutions, and bonds that I laid myself under by a kind of vows to God, I was brought wholly to break off all former wicked ways, and all ways of known outward sin, and to apply myself to seek my salvation, and practice the duties of religion; but without that kind of affection and delight that I had formerly experienced. My concern now wrought more by inward struggles and conflicts and self-reflections. I made seeking my salvation the main business of my life. But yet it seems to me I sought after a miserable manner, which has made me sometimes since to question whether ever it issued in that which was saving; being ready to doubt whether such miserable seeking was ever succeeded. But yet I was brought to seek salvation in a manner that I never was before. I felt a spirit to part with all things in the world for an interest in Christ. My concern continued and prevailed, with many exercising thoughts and inward struggles; but yet it never seemed to be proper to express my concern that I had by the name of terror.

From my childhood up, my mind had been wont to be full of objections against the doctrine of God's sovereignty in choosing whom he would to eternal life, and rejecting whom he pleased, leaving them eternally to perish, and be everlastingly tormented in hell. It used to appear like a horrible doctrine to me. But I remember the time very well, when I seemed to be convinced, and fully satisfied, as to this sovereignty of God, and his justice in thus eternally disposing of men according to his sovereign pleasure. But never could give an account, how or by what means I was thus convinced; not in the least imaging in the time of it, nor a long time after that there was any extraordinary influence of God's Spirit in it; but only that now I saw further, and my reason apprehended the justice and reasonableness of it. However, my mind rested in it, and it put an end to all those cavils and objections that had till then abode with me all the preceding part of my life. And there has been a wonderful alteration in my mind, with respect to the doctrine of God's sovereignty, from that day to this, so that I scarce ever have found so much as the rising of an objection against God's sovereignty, in the most absolute sense, in showing mercy to whom he will show mercy, and hardening and eternally damning whom he will. God's absolute sovereignty and justice, with respect to salvation and damnation, is what my mind seems to rest assured of, as much as of any thing that I see with my eyes; at least it is so at times. But I have often times since that first conviction had quite another kind of sense of God's sovereignty than I had then. I have often since, not only had conviction, but a *delightful* conviction. The doctrine of God's sovereignty has very often appeared, an exceeding pleasant, bright and sweet doctrine to me: and absolute sovereignty is what I love to ascribe to God. But my first conviction was not with this.

This first that I remember that ever I found any thing of that sort of inward, sweet delight in God and divine things that I have lived much in since, was on reading those words, 1 Timothy 1:17, *"Now unto the King eternal, immortal, invisible, the only wise God, be honour and glory for ever, and ever, Amen."* As I read the words there came into my soul, and was as it were diffused through it a sense of the glory of the Divine Being, a new sense quite different from any thing I ever experienced before. Never any words of Scripture seemed to me as these words did. I thought with myself, how excellent a Being that was, and how happy I should be if I might enjoy that God, and be wrapped up to

God in heaven, and be as it were swallowed up in him. I kept saying and as it were singing over these words of Scripture to myself; and went to prayer, to pray to God that I might enjoy him, and prayed in a manner quite different from what I used to do, with a new sort of affection. But it never came into my thought, that there was any thing spiritual or of a saving nature in this.

From about that time I began to have a new kind of apprehensions and ideas of Christ, and the work of redemption, and the glorious way of salvation by him. I had an inward, sweet sense of these things that at times came into my heart; and my soul was led away in pleasant views and contemplations of them. And my mind was greatly engaged to spend my time in reading and meditating on Christ, and the beauty and excellency of his person, and the lovely way of salvation by free grace in him. I found no books so delightful to me as those that treated of these subjects. Those words, Canticles* 2:1 used to be abundantly with me, *"I am the Rose of Sharon, and the Lily of the valleys."* The words seemed to me sweetly to represent the loveliness and beauty of Jesus Christ. And the whole Book of Canticles used to be pleasant to me; and I used to be much in reading it about that time; and found, from time to time, an inward sweetness that used, as it were, to carry me away in my contemplations; in what I know not how to express otherwise, than by a calm, sweet abstraction of soul from all the concerns of this world; and a kind of vision or fixed ideas and imaginations of being alone in the mountains or some solitary wilderness far from all mankind, sweetly conversing with Christ, and wrapped and swallowed up in God. The sense of divine things would often of a sudden, as it were, kindle up a sweet burning in my heart; an ardor of my soul that I know not how to express.

---

* This is another name for the *Song of Solomon.* HRR

Not long after I first began to experience these things, I gave an account to my father of some things that had passed in my mind. I was pretty much affected by the discourse we had together; and when the discourse was ended I walked abroad alone, in a solitary place in my father's pasture, for contemplation. And as I was walking there, and looked up on the sky and clouds, there came into my mind so sweet a sense of the glorious majesty and grace of God that I know not how to express. I seemed to see them both in a sweet conjunction: majesty and meekness joined together; it was a sweet and gentle, and holy majesty; and also a majestic meekness; an awful sweetness; a high and great, and holy gentleness.

After this my sense of divine things gradually increased, and became more and more lively, and had more of that inward sweetness. The appearance of every thing was altered, there seemed to be, as it were, a calm, sweet cast or appearance of divine glory in almost every thing. God's excellency, his wisdom, his purity and love seemed to appear in every thing; in the sun, moon and stars; in the clouds and blue sky; in the grass, flowers, trees; in the water and all nature; which used greatly to fix my mind. I often used to sit and view the moon for a long time; and so in the day time spent much time in viewing the clouds and sky, to behold the sweet glory of God in these things; in the mean time singing forth, with a low voice, my contemplations of the Creator and Redeemer. And scarce any thing among all the works of nature were so sweet to me as thunder and lightning; formerly nothing had been so terrible to me. I used to be a person uncommonly terrified with thunder, and it used to strike me with terror when I saw a thunder storm rising. But now, on the contrary, it rejoiced me. I felt God at the first appearance of a thunder storm; and used to take the opportunity, at such times, to fix myself to view the clouds, and see the lightnings play, and hear the majestic and awful voice of God's thunder, which often times was exceeding entertaining, leading me to sweet contemplations of my great and glorious God; and while I viewed, used to spend my time, as it always seemed natural to me to sing or chant forth my meditations; to speak my thoughts in soliloquies, and speak with a singing voice.

I felt then a great satisfaction as to my good estate; but that did not content me. I had vehement longings of soul after God and Christ, and after more holiness, wherewith my heart seemed to be full and ready to break; which often brought to my mind the word of the Psalmist, Psalm 119:20, *"My soul breaketh for the longing it hath."* I often felt a mourning and lamenting in my heart that I had not turned to God sooner, that I might have had more time to grow in grace. My mind was greatly fixed on divine things; I was almost perpetually in the contemplation of them. Spent most of my time in thinking of divine things, year after year; and used to spend abundance of my time in walking alone in the woods, and solitary places for meditation, soliloquy and prayer, and converse with God; and it was always my manner at such times to sing forth my contemplations; and was almost constantly in ejaculatory prayer wherever I was. Prayer seemed to be natural to me, as the breath by which the inward burnings of my heart had vent.

The delights which I now felt in things of religion were of an exceeding different kind from those fore-mentioned, that I had when I was a boy. They were totally of another kind; and what I then had no more notion or idea of, than one born blind has of pleasant and beautiful colors. They were of a more inward, pure, soul animating and refreshing nature. Those former delights never reached the heart, and did not arise from any sight of the divine excellency of the things of God, or any taste of the soul satisfying and life giving good there is in them.

My sense of divine things seemed gradually to increase, until I went to preach at New York, which was about a year and a half after they began. While I was there I felt them very sensibly, in a much higher degree than I had done before. My longings after God and holiness were much increased. Pure and humble, holy and heavenly Christianity appeared exceeding amiable to me. I felt in me a burning desire to be in every thing a complete Christian; and conformed to the blessed image of Christ; and that I might live in all things, according to the pure, sweet and blessed rules of the gospel. I had an eager thirsting after progress in these things. My longings, after it put me upon pursuing and pressing after them. It was my continual strife day and night, and constant inquiry, how I should be more holy and live more holily, and more becoming a child of God and disciple of Christ. I sought an increase of grace and holiness, and that I might live a holy life with vastly more earnestness than ever I sought grace before I had it. I used to be continually examining myself, and studying and contriving for likely ways and means, how I should live holily, with far greater diligence and earnestness than ever I pursued any thing in my life, but with too great a dependence on my own strength; which afterwards proved a great damage to me. My experience had not then taught me, as it has done since my extreme feebleness and impotence, every manner of way; and the innumerable and bottomless depths of secret corruption and deceit that there was in my heart. However, I went on with my eager pursuit after more holiness and sweet conformity to Christ.

The heaven I desired was a heaven of holiness; to be with God, and to spend my eternity in divine love and holy communion with Christ. My mind was very much taken up with contemplations on heaven, and the enjoyments of those there; and living there in perfect holiness, humility and love. And it used at that time to appear a great part of the happiness of heaven that there the saints could express their love to Christ. It appeared to me a great clog and hindrance and burden to me that what I felt within I could not express to God, and give vent to as I desired. The inward ardor of my soul seemed to be hindered and pent up, and could not freely flame out as it would. I used often to think, how in heaven this sweet principle should freely and fully vent and express itself. Heaven appeared to me exceeding delightful as a world of love. It appeared to me that all happiness consisted in living in pure, humble, heavenly, divine love.

I remember the thoughts I used then to have of holiness. I remember I then said sometimes to myself, I do certainly know that I love holiness, such as the gospel prescribes. It appeared to me there was nothing in it but what was ravishingly lovely. It appeared to me, to be the highest beauty and amiableness, above all other beauties that it was a *divine* beauty, far purer than any thing here upon earth, and that every thing else was like mire, filth and defilement in comparison of it.

Holiness, as I then wrote down some of my contemplations on it, appeared to me to be of a sweet, pleasant, charming, serene, calm nature. It seemed to me it brought an inexpressible purity, brightness, peacefulness and ravishment to the soul; and that it made the soul like a field or garden of God, with all manner of pleasant flowers; that is all pleasant, delightful and undisturbed; enjoying a sweet calm, and the gently vivifying beams of the sun. The soul of a true Christian, as I then wrote my meditations, appeared like such a little white flower, as we see in the spring of the year, low and humble on the ground, opening its bosom to receive the pleasant beams of the sun's glory; rejoicing, as it were, in a calm rapture; diffusing around a sweet fragrance; standing peacefully and lovingly in the midst of other flowers round about; all in like manner opening their bosoms to drink in the light of the sun.

There was no part of creature holiness that I then, and at other times, had so great a sense of the loveliness of, as humility, brokenness of heart and poverty of spirit; and there was nothing that I had such a spirit to long for. My heart, as it were, panted after this, to lie low before God and in the dust; that I might be nothing, and that God might be all; that I might become as a little child.

While I was there at New York I sometimes was much affected with reflections on my past life, considering how late it was before I began to be truly religious, and how wickedly I had lived till then; and once so as to weep abundantly, and for a considerable time together.

On January 12, 1722-3, I made a solemn dedication of myself to God, and wrote it down; giving up myself and all that I had to God, to be for the future in no respect my own, to act as one that had no right to himself in any respect. And solemnly vowed to take God for my whole portion and felicity, looking on nothing else as any part of my happiness, nor acting as if it were , and his law for the constant rule of my obedience; engaging to fight with all my might against the world, the flesh and the devil to the end of my life. But have reason to be infinitely humbled, when I consider how much I have failed of answering my obligation.

I had then abundance of sweet religious conversation in the family where I lived, with Mr. John Smith and his pious mother. My heart was knit in affection to those, in whom were appearances of true piety; and I could bear the thoughts of no other companions, but such as were holy, and the disciples of the blessed Jesus.

I had great longings for the advancement of Christ's kingdom in the world. My sacred prayer used to be in great part taken up in praying for it. If I heard the least hint of any thing that happened in any part of the world that appeared to me, in some respect or other, to have a favorable aspect on the interest of Christ's kingdom, my soul eagerly caught at it; and it would much animate and refresh me. I used to be earnest to read public news letters, mainly for that end; to see if I could not find some news favorable to the interest of religion in the world.

I very frequently used to retire into a solitary place, on the banks of the Hudson River, at some distance from the city, for contemplation on divine things, and secret converse with God; and had many sweet hours there. Sometimes Mr.

Smith and I walked there together to converse on the things of God; and our conversation used much to turn on the advancement of Christ's kingdom in the world, and the glorious things that God would accomplish for his church in the latter days.

I had then, and at other times, the greatest delight in the Holy Scriptures of any book whatsoever. Often times in reading it, every word seemed to touch my heart. I felt a harmony between something in my heart, and those sweet and powerful words. I seemed often to see so much light exhibited by every sentence, and such a refreshing ravishing food communicated, that I could not get along in reading. Used often times to dwell long on one sentence, to see the wonders contained in it; and yet almost every sentence seemed to be full of wonders.

I came away from New York in the month of April 1723, and had a most bitter parting with Madam Smith and her son. My heart seemed to sink within me at leaving the family and city, where I had enjoyed so many sweet and pleasant days. I went from New York to Wethersfield by water. As I sailed away, I kept sight of the city as long as I could; and when I was out of sight of it, it would affect me much to look that way, with a kind of melancholy mixed with sweetness. However, that night after this sorrowful parting, I was greatly comforted in God at Westchester, where we went ashore to lodge; and had a pleasant time ... all the voyage to Saybrook. It was sweet to me to think of meeting dear Christians in heaven, where we should never part more. At Saybrook we went ashore to lodge on Saturday, and there kept Sabbath; where I had a sweet and refreshing season walking alone in the fields.

After I came home to Windsor, remained much in a like frame of mind as I had been in at New York, but only sometimes felt my heart ready to sink with the thoughts of my friends at New York. And my refuge and support was in contemplations on the heavenly state; as I find in my Diary of May 1, 1723. It was my comfort to think of that state, where there is fullness of joy; where reigns heavenly, sweet, calm and delightful love without alloy; where there are continually the dearest expressions of this love; where is the enjoyment of the persons loved, without ever parting; where these persons that appear so lovely in this world, will really be inexpressibly more lovely and full of love to us. And how sweetly will the mutual lovers join together to sing the praises of God and the Lamb! How full will it fill us with joy to think that this enjoyment, these sweet exercises, will never cease or come to an end, but will last to all eternity!

Continued much in the same frame in the general that I had been in at New York, till I went to New Haven to live there as Tutor of the College[§]; having one special season of uncommon sweetness; particularly once at Boston, in a journey from Boston, walking out alone in the fields. After I went to New Haven I sunk in religion; my mind being diverted from my eager and violent pursuits after holiness, by some affairs that greatly perplexed and distracted my mind.

In September 1725, was taken ill at New Haven; and endeavoring to go home to Windsor was so ill at the North Village that I could go no further; where I lay sick for about a quarter of a year. And in this sickness God was pleased to visit me again with the sweet influences of his Spirit. My mind was greatly engaged there on divine, pleasant contemplations and longings of soul. I observed that those who watched with me would often be looking out for the morning, and seemed to wish for it; which brought to my mind those words of the Psalmist, which my soul with sweetness made its own language, *"My soul waiteth for the Lord, more than they that watch for the morning; I say, more than they that watch for the morning."*[*] And when the light of the morning came, and the beams of the sun came in

---

[§] Yale College
[*] Psalm 130:6

64

at the windows, it refreshed my soul from one morning to another. It seemed to me to be some image of the sweet light of God's glory.

I remember, about that time, I used greatly to long for the conversion of some that I was concerned with. It seemed to me, I could gladly honor them, and with delight be a servant to them, and lie at their feet, if they were but truly holy.

But some time after this I was again greatly diverted in my mind, with some temporal concerns that exceedingly took up my thoughts, greatly to the wounding of my soul; and went on through various exercises, that it would be tedious to relate, that gave me much more experience of my own heart than ever I had before.

Since I came to this town (Northampton), I have often had sweet complacency in God, in view of his glorious perfections, and the excellency of Jesus Christ. God has appeared to me a glorious and loving being, chiefly on the account of his holiness. The holiness of God has always appeared to me the most lovely of all his attributes. The doctrines of God's absolute sovereignty and free grace, in showing mercy to whom he would show mercy, and man's absolute dependence on the operations of God's Holy Spirit, have very often appeared to me as sweet and glorious doctrines. These doctrines have been much my delight. God's sovereignty has ever appeared to me as a great part of his glory. It has often been sweet to me to go to God, and adore him as a sovereign God, and ask sovereign mercy of him.

I have loved the doctrines of the gospel; they have been to my soul like green pastures. The gospel has seemed to me to be the richest treasure, the treasure that I have most desired, and longed that it might dwell richly in me. The way of salvation by Christ has appeared in a general way, glorious and excellent, and most pleasant and most beautiful. It has often seemed to me that it would in a great measure spoil heaven to receive it in any other way. That text has often been affecting and delightful to me, Isaiah 32:2, *"A man shall be as an hiding place from the wind, and a covert from the tempest...."*

It has often appeared sweet to me to be united to Christ; to have him for my head, and to be a member of his body; and also to have Christ for my teacher and prophet. I very often think with sweetness and longings, and pantings of the soul, of being a little child, taking hold of Christ, to be led by him through the wilderness of this world. That text, Matthew 18 at the beginning has often been sweet to me, *"Except ye be converted, and become as little children...."* [§] I love to think of coming to Christ, to receive salvation of him, poor in spirit and quite empty of self; humbly exalting him alone; cut entirely off from my root, and to grow into and out of Christ; to have God in Christ to be all in all; and to live by faith on the Son of God, a life of humble, unfeigned confidence in him. That Scripture has often been sweet to me, Psalm 115:1, *"Not unto us, O Lord, not unto us, but unto thy name give glory, for thy mercy, and for thy truth's sake."* And those words of Christ, Luke 10:21, *"In that hour Jesus rejoiced in spirit, and said, I thank thee, O Father, Lord of heaven and earth, that thou hast hid these things from the wise and prudent, and hast revealed them unto babes: even so, Father, for so it seemed good in thy sight."* That sovereignty of God that Christ rejoiced in, seemed to me to be worthy to be rejoiced in; and that rejoicing of Christ, seemed to me to show the excellency of Christ, and the spirit that he was of.

Sometimes only mentioning a single word causes my heart to burn within me; or only seeing the name of Christ, or the name of some attribute of God. And God has appeared glorious to me on account of the Trinity. It has made me have exalting thoughts of God, that he subsists in three persons, Father, Son and Holy Spirit.

[§] Matthew 18:3

The sweetest joys and delights I have experienced have not been those that have arisen from a hope of my own good estate, but in a direct view of the glorious things of the gospel. When I enjoy this sweetness, it seems to carry me above the thoughts of my own safe estate; it seems at such times a loss that I cannot bear to take off my eye from the glorious, pleasant object I behold without me to turn my eye in upon myself, and my own good estate.

My heart has been much on the advancement of Christ's kingdom in the world. The histories of the past advancement of Christ's kingdom have been sweet to me. When I have read histories of past ages, the pleasantest things in all my reading has been to read of the kingdom of Christ being promoted. And when I have expected in my reading to come to any such thing, I have lotted* upon it all the way as I read. And my mind has been much entertained and delighted with the Scripture promises and prophecies of the future glorious advancement of Christ's kingdom on earth.

I have sometimes had a sense of the excellent fullness of Christ, and his meetness and suitableness as a Saviour; whereby he has appeared to me far above all, the chief of ten thousands; and his blood and atonement has appeared sweet, and his righteousness sweet; which is always accompanied with an ardency of spirit, and inward strugglings, breathings and groanings that cannot be uttered, to be emptied of myself and swallowed up in Christ.

Once, as I rode out into the woods for my health, *anno 1737*, and having lighted from my horse in a retired place, as my manner commonly has been, to walk for divine contemplation and prayer, I had a view that for me was extraordinary of the glory of the son of God, as Mediator between God and man; and his wonderful, great, full, pure

---

* "Lotted upon" or desired. To "lot upon" is to anticipate with fondness or desire. This was a colloquial phrase used in New England. HRR

and sweet grace, and love, and meek, and gentle condescension. This grace that appeared to me so calm and sweet appeared great above the heavens. The person of Christ appeared ineffably excellent, with an excellency great enough to swallow up all thought and conception, which continued, as near as I can judge, about an hour, which kept me the greater part of the time in a flood of tears and weeping aloud. I felt withal an ardency of soul to be what I know not otherwise how to express, than to be emptied and annihilated; to lie in the dust, and to be full of Christ alone; to love him with a holy and pure love; to trust in him; to live upon him; to serve and follow him, and to be totally wrapped up in the fullness of Christ; and to be perfectly sanctified and made pure with a divine and heavenly purity. I have several other times had views very much of the same nature, and that have had the same effects.

I have many times had a sense of the glory of the Third Person of the Trinity in his office of Sanctifier, in his holy operations, communicating divine light and life to the soul. God, in the communications of his Holy Spirit has appeared as an infinite fountain of divine glory and sweetness, being full and sufficient to fill and satisfy the soul; pouring forth itself in sweet communications, like the sun in its glory, sweetly and pleasantly diffusing light and life.

I have sometimes had an affecting sense of the excellency of the Word of God, as a word of life; as the light of life; a sweet, excellent, life-giving word; accompanied with a thirsting after that word, that it might dwell richly in my heart.

I have often, since I lived in this town, had very affecting views of my own sinfulness and vileness, very frequently so as to hold me in a kind of loud weeping, sometimes for a considerable time together, so that I have often been forced to shut myself up. I have had a vastly greater sense of my own wickedness, and the badness of my heart since my conversion than ever I had before. It has often appeared to me that if God should mark iniquity against me I should appear the very worst of all mankind; of all that have been since the beginning of the world to this time, and that I should have by far the lowest place in hell. When others, that have come to talk with me about their soul concerns, have expressed the sense they have had of their own wickedness, by saying that it seemed to them that they were as bad as the devil himself, I thought their expressions seemed exceeding faint and feeble to represent my wickedness. I thought I should wonder that they should content themselves with such expressions as these, if I had any reason to imagine that their sin bore any proportion to mine. It seemed to me, I should wonder at myself, if I should express *my* wickedness in such feeble terms as they did.

My wickedness, as I am in myself, has long appeared to me perfectly ineffable, and infinitely swallowing up all thought and imagination, like an infinite deluge or infinite mountains over my head. I know not how to express better what my sins appear to me to be, than by heaping infinite upon infinite, and multiplying infinite by infinite. I go about very often, for this many years, with these expressions in my mind and in my mouth, "Infinite upon infinite—infinite upon infinite!" When I look into my heart and take a view of my wickedness, it looks like an abyss infinitely deeper than hell. And it appears to me that were it not for free grace, exalted and raised up to the infinite height of all the fullness and glory of the great Jehovah, and the arm of his power, and in all the glory of his sovereignty, I should appear sunk down in my sins infinitely below hell itself, far beyond sight of every thing, but the piercing eye of God's grace, that can pierce even down to such a depth, and to the bottom of such an abyss.

And yet I am not in the least inclined to think that I have a greater conviction of sin than ordinary. It seems to me, my conviction of sin is exceeding small and faint. It appears to me enough to amaze me, that I have no more sense of my sin. I know certainly that I have very little sense of my sinfulness. That my sins appear to me so great, do not seem to me to be, because I have so much more conviction of sin than other Christians, but because I am so much worse, and have so much more wickedness to be convinced of. When I have had these turns of weeping and crying for my sins, I thought I knew in the time of it that my repentance was nothing to my sin.

I have greatly longed of late for a broken heart, and to lie low before God. And when I asked for humility of God, I cannot bear the thoughts of being no more humble than other Christians. It seems to me, that though their degrees of humility may be suitable for them, yet it would be a vile self-exaltation in me not to be the lowest in humility of all mankind. Others speak of their longing to be humbled to the dust. Though that may be a proper expression for them, I always think for myself that I ought to be humbled down below hell. 'Tis an expression that has long been natural for me to use in prayer to God. I ought to lie infinitely low before God.

It is affecting to me to think how ignorant I was, when I was a young Christian, of the bottomless, infinite depths of wickedness, pride, hypocrisy and deceit, left in my heart.

I have vastly a greater sense of my universal, exceeding dependence on God's grace and strength, and mere good pleasure of late, than I used formerly to have, and have experienced more of an abhorrence of my own righteousness. The thought of any comfort or joy arising in me on any consideration or reflection on my own amiableness or any of my performances or experiences or any goodness of heart or life is nauseous and detestable to me. And yet I am greatly afflicted with a proud and self-righteous spirit, much more sensibly than I used to be formerly. I see that serpent rising and putting forth its head continually, everywhere, all around me.

Though it seems to me that, in some respects, I was a far better Christian for two or three years after my first conversion than I am now, and lived in a more constant delight and pleasure, yet, of late years, I have had a more full and constant sense of the absolute sovereignty of God, and a delight in that sovereignty; and have had more of a sense of the glory of Christ, as a Mediator, as revealed in the gospel. On one Saturday night, in particular, had a particular discovery of the excellency of the gospel of Christ above all other doctrines, so that I could not but say to myself, "This is my chosen light, my chosen doctrine;" and of Christ, "This is my chosen Prophet." It appeared to me to be sweet, beyond all expression to follow Christ, and to be taught, and enlightened, and instructed by him; to learn of him, and live to him.

Another Saturday night, January 1738-9, had such a sense how sweet and blessed a thing it was to walk in the way of duty, to do that which was right and meet to be done, and agreeable to the holy mind of God, that it caused me to break forth into a kind of a loud weeping, which held me some time, so that I was forced to shut myself up and fasten the doors. I could not but as it were cry out, "How happy are they which do that which is right in the sight of God! They are blessed indeed, they are the happy ones!" I had at the same time a very affecting sense how meet, and suitable it was that God should govern the world, and order all things according to his own pleasure; and I rejoiced in it that God reigned, and that his will was done.

The Life and Character of Mr. Jonathan Edwards

~~~~~~~~
========

PART III

Containing a History of his Life, from his Entering on
the Work of the Ministry unto his Death.

***

SECTION I

HIS GENERAL MANNER OF LIFE

Mr. Edwards made a secret of his private devotion,
and therefore it cannot be particularly known; though there
is much evidence that he was punctual, constant and
frequent in secret prayer; and often kept days of fasting and
prayer in secret, and set apart time for serious devout
meditations on spiritual and eternal things, as part of his
religious exercise in secret. It appears by his Diary that in
his youth he determined to attend secret prayer more than
twice a day, when circumstances would allow. He was, so
far as can be known, much on his knees in secret, and in
devout reading God's Word and meditation upon it. And
his constant, solemn converse with God in these exercises
of secret religion made his face, and it were, to shine before
others. His appearance, his countenance, words and whole
demeanor (though without any thing of affected grimace
and sour austerity), was attended with a seriousness, gravity
and solemnity, which was the natural, genuine indication
and expression of a deep, abiding sense of divine things on
his mind, and of his living constantly in the fear of God.

Agreeable to his Resolutions, he was very careful and
abstemious* in eating and drinking, as doubtless it was

---

* *Abstemious* means to be sparing in diet or to restrict the free use
of food. HRR

73

necessary so great a student and a person of so delicate and tender a bodily make as he was, should be, in order to be comfortable and useful. When he had, by careful observation, found what kind and what quantity of diet best suited his constitution, and rendered him most fit to pursue his work, he was very strict and exact in complying with it; and in this respect *lived by rule*; and herein constantly practiced great self-denial, which he also did in his constant early rising, in order to redeem time for his study. He used himself to rise by four or between four and five in the morning.

Though he was of a tender and delicate constitution, yet few students are capable of close application more hours in a day than he. He commonly spent thirteen hours every day in his study. His most usual diversion, in summer, was riding on horseback and walking. He would commonly, unless diverted by company, ride two or three miles after dinner to some lonely grove, where he would dismount and walk a while. At which times he generally carried his pen and ink with him to note any thought that should be suggested, which he chose to retain and pursue, as what promised some light on any important subject. In the winter he was wont almost daily to take an ax and chop wood moderately, for the space of half an hour or more.

He had an uncommon thirst for knowledge; in the pursuit of which he spared no cost or pains. He read all the books, especially books of divinity that he could come at, from which he could hope to get any help in his pursuit of knowledge. And in this, he confined not himself to authors of any particular sect or denomination; yea, took much pains to come at the books of the most noted writers, who advance a scheme of divinity most contrary to his own principles. But he studied the Bible more than all others books and more than most other divines do. His uncommon acquaintance with the Bible appears in his sermons, and in most of his publications; and his great pains in studying it are manifest in his manuscript notes upon it; of which a more particular account may be given hereafter. He took his religious principles from the Bible, and not from any human system or body of divinity. Though his principles were *Calvinistic*, yet he called no man father. He thought and judged for himself, and was truly very much of an original. This is evident by what he published in his life time, and is yet more so by his manuscripts. Many volumes of which he has left; and the reader may expect a more particular account of them in the sequel. For reading was not the only method he took to improve his mind; but he did this much by writing; without which it is probable no student can make improvements to the best advantage. Agreeable to Resolution 11 he applied himself with all his mind to find out the truth; he searched for understanding and knowledge, as for silver and digged for it, as for hid treasures. Every thought on any subject which appeared to him worth pursuing and preserving, he pursued, as far as he then could, with his pen in his hand. Thus he was all his days, like the busy bee, collecting from every opening flower, and storing up a stock of knowledge, which was indeed sweet to him as the honey and the honey comb. And as he advanced in years and in knowledge, his pen was more and more employed, and his manuscripts grew much faster on his hands.

He was thought by some, who had but a slight acquaintance with him, to be stiff and unsociable; but this was owing to want of better acquaintance. He was not a man of many words indeed, and was somewhat reserved among strangers, and those on whose candor and friendship he did not know he could rely. And this was probably owing to two things: *first,* the strict guard he set over his tongue from his youth, which appears by his Resolutions, taking great care never to use it in any way that might prove mischievous to any; never to *sin with his tongue*; nor to improve it in idle, trivial and impertinent talk, which generally makes up a great part of the conversation of those who are full of words in all companies. He was sensible that *"in the multitude of words there wanteth not sin;"*[§] and therefore refrained his lips, and habituated himself to *think* before he spoke, and to propose some good end even in all his words; which led him to be above many others, agreeable to St. James' advice, *"slow to speak."*[*] *Secondly*, this was in part the effect of his bodily constitution. He possessed but a comparative small stock of animal life; his animal spirits that would be necessary in order to make him what would be called, an affable facetious gentleman in all companies. They who have a great flow of animal spirits, and so can speak with more ease and less expense, may doubtless lawfully practice free conversation in all companies for a lower end (e.g. to please and render themselves acceptable), than he, who has not such a stock to expend upon. It becomes *him* to reserve what he has for higher and more important service. Besides, the want of animal spirits lays a man under a *natural* inability to that freedom of conversation at all times, and in whatever company he is, which those of more life naturally go into; and the greatest degree of sociable disposition, humility and benevolence will not remove this obstacle.

He was not forward to enter into any dispute among strangers, and in companies where were persons of different sentiments; as he was sensible that such disputes are generally unprofitable, and often sinful, and of bad consequence; and he thought he could dispute to the best advantage with his pen in his hand; yet he was always free to give his sentiments on any subject proposed to him, and remove any difficulties or objections offered by way of inquiry, as lying in the way of what he looked upon to be the truth. But how groundless the imputation of *stiff* and *unsociable* was his known and tried friends best knew.

[§] Proverbs 10:19
[*] James 1:19

76

They always found him easy of access, kind and condescending; and though not talkative, yet affable and free. Among such whose candor and friendship he had experienced he threw off the reserve, and was most open and free; quite patient of contradiction, while the utmost opposition was made to his sentiments, that could be by any plausible arguments or objections. And, indeed, he was on all occasions quite sociable and free with all who had any special business with him.

In his conduct in his family he practiced that conscientious exactness which was perspicuous in all his ways. He maintained a great esteem and regard for his amiable and excellent consort. Much of the tender and kind was expressed in his conversation with her and conduct towards her. He was wont frequently to admit her into his study, at least once a day, unless something extraordinary prevented. The time in which this used to be commonly attended was just before going to bed, after prayers in the family. As he rose very early himself, he was wont to have his family up in season in the morning; after which, before the family entered on the business of the day, he attended on family prayers; when a chapter in the Bible was read, commonly by candle light in the winter; upon which he asked his children questions according to their age and capacity; and took occasion to explain some passages in it or enforce any duty recommended, etc. as he thought most proper.

He was careful and thorough in the government of his children; and, as a consequence of this, they reverenced, esteemed and loved him. He took special care to begin his government of them in season. When they first discovered any considerable degree of will and stubbornness, he would attend to them till he had thoroughly subdued them and brought them to submit. And such prudent thorough discipline, exercised with the greatest calmness and commonly without striking a blow, being repeated once or twice, was generally sufficient for that child; and effectually established his parental authority, and produced a cheerful obedience ever after.

He kept a watchful eye over his children that he might admonish them of the *first* wrong step, and direct them in the right way. He took opportunities to treat with them in his study, singly and particularly about their own soul's concerns; and to give them warning, exhortation and direction as he saw occasion. He took much pains to instruct them in the principles of religion in which he made use of the *Assembly's Shorter Catechism*: not merely by taking care that they learned it by heart, but by leading them into an understanding of the doctrines therein taught, by asking them questions on each answer, and explaining it to them. His usual time to attend this was on the evening before the Sabbath. And, as he believed that the Sabbath or holy time began at sunset the evening before the day, he ordered his family to finish all their secular business by that time or before; when they were all called together, and a psalm was sung and prayer attended, as an introduction to ... sanctifying the Sabbath. This care and exactness effectually prevented that intruding on holy time, by attending on secular business too common in families where the evening before the Sabbath is pretended to be observed.

He was a great enemy to young people's unseasonable company keeping and frolicking, as he looked upon it as a great means of corrupting and ruining youth. And he thought the excuse many parents make for tolerating their children in it (viz. that it is the custom, and others children practice it, which renders it difficult, and even impossible to restrain theirs), was insufficient and frivolous; and manifested a great degree of stupidity on supposition the practice was hurtful and pernicious to their souls. And when some of his children grew up he found no difficulty in restraining them from this pernicious practice; but they cheerfully complied with the will of their parents herein. He allowed not his children to be from home after nine o'clock at night, when they went abroad to see their friends and companions; neither were they allowed to sit up much after that time in his own house, when any came to make them a visit. If any gentleman desired acquaintance with his daughters, after handsomely introducing himself, by properly consulting the parents, he was allowed all proper opportunity for it, and a room and fire if needed: but must not intrude on the proper hours of rest and sleep, nor the religion and order of the family.

He had a strict and inviolable regard to justice in all his dealings with his neighbors, and was very careful to provide for things honest in the sight of all men; so that scarcely a man had any dealings with him that was not conscious of his uprightness. He appeared to have a sacred regard to truth in his words, both in promises and narrations, agreeable to his Resolutions. This doubtless was one reason why he was not so full of words as many are: no man feared to rely on his veracity.

He was cautious in choosing his intimate friends, and therefore had not many that might properly be called such; but to them he showed himself friendly in a peculiar manner. He was indeed a faithful friend, and able above most others to keep a secret. To them he discovered himself more than to others; led them into his views and ends in his conduct in particular instances; by which they had abundant evidence that he well understood human nature, and that his general reserve, and many particular instances of his conduct, which a stranger might impute to ignorance of men, were really owing to his uncommon knowledge of mankind.

His conversation with his friends was always savory and profitable: in this he was remarkable and almost singular. He was not wont to spend his time with them in scandal, evil speaking and back biting or in foolish jesting, idle chat and telling stories; but his mouth was that of the just, which brings forth wisdom, and his lips disperses knowledge. His tongue was as the pen of a ready writer, while he conversed about important, heavenly, divine

79

things, which his heart was so full of, in such a natural and free manner, as to be most entertaining and instructive; so that none of his friends could enjoy his company without instruction and profit, unless it was by their own fault.

His great benevolence to mankind discovered itself among other ways, by the uncommon regard he showed to liberality and charity to the poor and distressed. He was much in recommending this, both in his public discourses and private conversation. He often declared it to be his opinion that professed Christians, in these days, are greatly deficient in this duty, and much more so than in most other parts of external Christianity. He often observed how much this is spoken of, recommended and encouraged in the Holy Scripture, especially in the New Testament. And it was his opinion that every particular church ought, by frequent and liberal contributions to maintain a public stock that might be ready for the poor and necessitous members of that church; and that the principal business of deacons is to take care of the poor in the faithful and judicious distribution and improvement of the church's temporals lodged in their hands. And he did not content himself with only recommending charity to others, but practiced it much himself; though according to his Master's advice, he took great care to conceal his deeds of charity; by which means, doubtless most of his alms deeds will be unknown till the resurrection, which if known would prove him to be as great an instance of charity as any that can be produced in this age. This is not mere conjecture, but is evident many ways. He was forward to give on all public occasions of charity; though, when it could properly be done, he always concealed the sum given. And some instances of his giving more privately have accidentally come to the knowledge of others, in which his liberality appeared in a very extraordinary degree. One of the instances was this: upon his hearing that a poor obscure man, whom he never saw or any of his kindred, was by an extraordinary bodily disorder brought to great straits, he, unasked, gave a considerable sum to a friend to be delivered to the distressed person; having first required a promise of him that he would let neither the person, who was the object of his charity, nor any one else know by whom it was given. This may serve both as an instance of his extraordinary charity, and of his great care to conceal it.*

Mr. Edwards had the most universal character of a good preacher of almost any minister in this age. There were but few that heard him, who did not call him a good preacher; however, they might dislike his religious principles, and be much offended at the same truths when delivered by others; and most admired him above all that ever they heard. His eminency as a preacher seems to be owing to the following things:

First, the great pains he took in composing his sermons, especially in the first part of his life. As by his early rising and constant attention to his study, he had more time than most others; so he spent more time in making his sermons. He wrote most of his sermons all out, for near twenty years after he first began to preach, though he did not wholly confine himself to his notes in his delivering them.

Secondly, his great acquaintance with divinity, his study and knowledge of the Bible; his extensive and universal knowledge, and great clearness of thought, enabled him to handle every subject with great judgment and propriety, and to bring out of his treasury things new and old. Every subject he handled was instructive, plain, entertaining and profitable; which was much owing to his being master of the subject, and his great skill to treat it in a most natural, easy and profitable manner. None of his composures were dry speculations or unmeaning harangues

---

* As both the giver, and the object of his charity are dead, and all the ends of the proposed secrecy are answered, it is thought not inconsistent with the above mentioned promise to make known the fact, as it is here related. Samuel Hopkins

or words without ideas. When he dwelt on those truths which are much controverted and opposed by many, which was often the case, he would set them in such a natural and easy light, and every sentiment from step to step would drop from his lips attended with such clear and striking evidence, both from Scripture and reason, as even to force the assent of every attentive hearer.

Thirdly, his excellency as a preacher was very much the effect of his great acquaintance with his own heart, his inward sense and high relish of divine truths; and the high exercise of true experimental religion. This gave him a great insight into human nature; he knew what was in man, both the saint and the sinner. This helped him to skill, to lay truth before the mind, so as not only to convince the judgment, but touch the heart and conscience; and enabled him to speak out of the abundance of his heart, when he knew and testified what he had seen and felt. This gave him a taste and discerning, without which he could not have been able to fill his sermons, as he did, with such striking, affecting sentiments all suited to solemnize, move and rectify the heart of the hearer. His sermons were well connected, not usually long and commonly a large part taken up in the improvement; which was closely connected with the subject, and consisted in sentiments naturally flowing from it.

But no description of his sermons will give the reader the idea of them, which they had, who sat under his preaching, or have even read some of his discourses, which are in print. There is a great number now in manuscript, which are probably as worthy the view of the public, and at least tend as much to instruct and quicken Christians as most that have been published in this century.

His appearance in the desk was with a good grace, and his delivery easy, natural and very solemn. He had not a strong, loud voice; but appeared with such gravity and solemnity, and spoke with such distinctness, clearness and precision; his words were so full of ideas, set in such a plain and striking light that few speakers have been so able to command the attention of an audience as he. His words often discovered a great degree of inward fervor, without much noise or external emotion, and fell with great weight on the minds of his hearers. He made but little motion of his head or hands in the desk; but spoke so as to discover the motion of his own heart, which tended in the most natural and effectual manner to move and affect others.

As he wrote his sermons out ... for many years, and always wrote a considerable part of most of his public discourses; so he carried his notes into the desk with him and read the most that he had written; yet he was not so confined to his notes, when he had written at large, but that if some thoughts were suggested while he was speaking, which did not occur when writing, and appeared to him pertinent and striking, he would deliver them; and that with as great propriety and fluency, and often with greater pathos, and attended with a more sensible good effect on his hearers than all he had written.

Though, as has been observed, he was wont to read so considerable a part of what he delivered, yet he was far from thinking this the best way of preaching in general; and looked upon his using his notes as much as he did a deficiency and infirmity; and, in the latter part of his life, was inclined to think it had been better if he had never accustomed himself to use his notes at all. It appeared to him that preaching wholly with out notes, agreeable to the custom in most Protestant countries, and what seemed evidently to have been the manner of the apostles and primitive ministers of the gospel, was by far the most natural way, and had the greatest tendency, on the whole, to answer the end of preaching; and supposed that none who had talents equal to the work of the ministry were incapable of speaking *memoriter*,[§] if he took suitable pains for this attainment from his youth. He would have the young

---

[§] *Memoriter* means to speak from memory or by heart. HRR

preacher write all his sermons, or at least most of them, out at large; and instead of reading those to his hearers take pains to commit them to memory. Which, though it would require a great deal of labor at first, yet would soon become easier by use, and help him to speak more correctly and freely, and be of great service to him all his days.

His prayers were indeed *extempore*. He was the farthest from any appearance of a form, as to his words and manner of expression, of almost any man. He was quite singular and inimitable in this by any who have not a spirit of real and undissembled devotion; yet he always expressed himself with decency and propriety. He appeared to have much of the grace and spirit of prayer; to pray with the spirit and with the understanding; and he performed this part of duty much to the acceptance and edification of those who joined with him. He was not wont, in ordinary cases, to be long in his prayers; an error which he observed was often hurtful to public and social prayer, as it tends rather to damp than promote true devotion.

He kept himself quite free from worldly cares. He gave himself wholly to the work of the ministry, and entangled not himself with the affairs of this life. He left the particular oversight and direction of the temporal concerns of his family almost entirely to Mrs. Edwards; who was better able than most of her sex to take the whole care of them on her hands. He was less acquainted with most of his temporal affairs than many of his neighbors; and seldom knew when and by whom his forage for winter was gathered in or how many milk cows he had; whence his table was furnished, etc.

He did not make it his custom to visit his people in their own houses unless he was sent for by the sick, or he heard that they were under some special affliction. Instead of visiting from house to house he used to preach frequently at private meetings in particular neighborhoods; and often called the young people and children to his own house, when he used to pray with them and treat with them in a

The Life and Character of Mr. Jonathan Edwards

manner suited to their years and circumstances; and he catechized the children in public every Sabbath in the summer. And he used sometimes to propose questions to particular young persons in writing for them to answer after a proper time given to them to prepare. In putting out these questions he endeavored to suit them to the age, genius and abilities of those to whom they were given. His questions were generally such as required but a short answer; and yet could not be answered without a particular knowledge of some historical part of the Scripture; and therefore led, and even obliged persons to study the Bible.

He did not neglect visiting his people from house to house, because he did not look upon it in ordinary cases, to be one part of the work of the gospel minister; but he supposed that ministers should, with respect to this consult their own talents and circumstances, and visit more or less according to the degrees in which they could hope hereby to promote the great ends of the gospel ministry. He observed that some ministers had a talent at entertaining and profiting by occasional visits among their people. They have words at will and a knack at introducing profitable, religious discourse, in a free, natural and, as it were, undersigned way. He supposed such had a call to spend a great deal of their time in visiting their people; but he looked on his talents to be quite otherwise. He was not able to enter into a free conversation with every person he met with, and in an easy manner turn it to what topic he pleased, without the help of others, and, as it may be, against their inclination. He therefore found that his visits of this kind must be in a great degree unprofitable. And as he was settled in a great town, it would take up a great part of his time to visit from house to house, which he thought he could spend in his study to much more valuable purposes, and so as much better to promote the great ends of his ministry. For it appeared to him that he could do the greatest good to souls, and most promote the interest of Christ by preaching and writing and conversing with persons under religious

85

impressions in his study; where he encouraged all such to repair; where they might be sure, in ordinary cases, to find him; and to be allowed easy access to him; and where they were treated with all desirable tenderness, kindness and familiarity. In times, therefore, of the outpouring of God's Spirit, and the revival of religion among his people, his study was thronged with persons to lay open their spiritual concerns to him, and seek his advice and direction: whom he received and conversed with, with great freedom and pleasure, and had the best opportunity to deal in the most particular manner with each one.

He was a skilful guide to souls under spiritual difficulties; and was therefore sought ... not only by his own people, but by many who lived scores of miles off. He became such an able guide, partly by his own experimental acquaintance with divine things, and unwearied study of God's Word, and partly by his having so much concern with souls under spiritual troubles; for he had not been settled in the work of the ministry many years before the Spirit of God was wonderfully poured out on his people, by which a great concern about their souls became almost universal, and a great number were hopefully the subjects of saving conversion. This was principally in the year 1734; a particular account of which has been written by him entitled *A Faithful Narrative of the Surprising Work of God in the Conversion of Many Hundred of Souls in Northampton*, which has been printed in England, Germany and America; to which the reader must be referred.

And there was another remarkable time of the outpouring of God's Spirit in the year 1740 and 1741, in which Northampton partook largely; though not exclusive of most parts of the land. Mr. Edwards in this time had to deal not only with his own people, but with multitudes of others. The hearing that the same things were at Northampton some years before, and the same Mr. Edwards had for knowledge, piety and a great acquaintance with experimental religion, naturally led both ministers and people, in almost all parts of New England, to look to him for direction and assistance in this extraordinary time. Being in this time earnestly solicited by the ministers and people of many places to come and preach among them, he went to many; though he was not able to gratify all who desired him; and his preaching was attended with great success.

And as many of the ministers and people in New England had been unacquainted with such things as then appeared, they were greatly exposed to *run wild*, as it were, and actually did, by the subtle temptations of the devil taking advantage of the ignorance and wickedness of men's hearts, go into great extremes, both as opposers and friends to the work of God. Mr. Edwards was greatly helpful by hid direction and assistance against the two opposite extremes, both in conversation, preaching and writing. His publications on this occasion were especially of great and extensive service. Of which it may be proper to give some account here.

The first is a sermon preached at New Haven, September 10, 1741, on *The Distinguishing Marks of a Work of the Spirit of God*, etc.

In the year 1742 he published a book of five parts entitled *Some Thoughts Concerning the Present Revival of Religion in New England, and the Way in Which it Ought to be Acknowledged and Promoted, etc.*

In the year 1746 he published a *Treatise on Religious Affections.* All which might be justly considered by the church of Christ as a voice behind them saying, *"This is the way, walk therein."* * Especially the last mentioned book, which has been esteemed by many the best that has been written on that subject; setting the distinction between true and false religion in the most clear and striking light.

---

* Isaiah 30:21

To the same purpose is *The Life of the Rev. Mr. David Brainerd, with Reflections and Observations Thereon*; published by Mr. Edwards in the year 1749.

Mr. Edwards was what by some is called a rigid Calvinist. Those doctrines of Calvinism, which have been most objected against and given the greatest offense, appeared to him as Scriptural, reasonable and important as any; and he thought that to give them up was in effect to give up all. And therefore he looked upon those who called themselves Calvinists that were for palliating the matter by, as it were, trimming off the knots of Calvinism, that they might conform it more to the taste of those who are most disposed to object against it, were really giving up and betraying the cause they pretended to espouse; and were paving the way, not only to Arminianism, but to Deism. For if these doctrines, in the whole length and breath of them were relinquished, he did not see where a man could set his foot down, with consistency and safety, short of Deism or even Atheism itself or rather universal Skepticism.

He judged that nothing was wanting but to have these doctrines properly stated and judiciously and well defended, in order to their appearing most agreeable to reason and common sense, as well as the doctrines of revelation; and that this therefore was the only effectual method to convince or silence and shame the opposers of them. All will be able to satisfy themselves of the truth of this by reading his treatise on *Justification*, and his two last books on *The Freedom of the Will*, and *Original Sin*.

In this view of things, he thought it of importance that ministers should be very critical in examining candidates for the ministry, with respect to their *principles* as well as their religious dispositions and morals. And on this account he met with considerable difficulty and opposition in some instances. His opinion was that an erroneous or unfaithful minister was likely to do more hurt than good to the church of Christ; and therefore he could not have any hand in introducing a man into the ministry unless he appeared *sound in the faith*, and manifested … a judgment of charity, a *disposition to be faithful*.

***

SECTION II

HIS DISMISSION FROM NORTHAMPTON, WITH THE OCCASION AND CIRCUMSTNACES OF IT

𝓜r. Edwards was very happy in the esteem and love of his people for many years, and there was the greatest prospect of his living and dying so. He was the last minister almost in New England that would have been pitched upon to be opposed and renounced by his people. But by what has come to pass, with respect to this, we have an instructive lesson on the instability of all human affairs, and the unreasonableness of trusting in man.

In the year 1744 Mr. Edwards was informed that some of the young persons in town, who were members of the church, had books in keeping, which they improved to promote lascivious and obscene discourse among the young people. And, upon inquiring, a number of persons were found to testify that they had heard one and another from time to time talk obscenely; as what they were led to by reading a book or books, which they had among them. Upon which Mr. Edwards thought the brethren of the church ought to look into the matter. And in order to introduce it he preached a sermon from Hebrews 12:15, 16, *"Looking diligently, lest any man fail of the grace of God, lest any root of bitterness springing up trouble you, and thereby many be defiled: lest there be any fornicator, or profane person as Esau...."* After the sermon he desired the brethren of the church to stay, and told them what information he had got; and proposed whether they thought proper to take any measures to examine into the matter. They, with one consent and much zeal, manifested it to be their opinion that it ought to be inquired into, and proceeded to choose a number of men to assist their pastor in examining into the affair. Upon which Mr. Edwards appointed the time for their meeting at his house; and then

90

read a catalogue of the names of young persons, whom he desired to come to his house at the same time. Some were the accused, and some witnesses; but it was not then declared of which number any particular person was.

When the names were published it appeared that there were but few, of the considerable families in town, to which none of the persons named, did belong or were nearly related. Whether this was the occasion of the alteration or not, before the day appointed came a great number of heads of families altered their minds (yea, many condemned what they had done, before they got home to their own houses), and declared, they did not think proper to proceed as they had done; that their children should not be called to an account in such a way for such things, etc. etc.; and the town was suddenly all on a blaze. This strengthened the hands of the accused, and some refused to appear, and others that did appear behaved unmannerly, and with a great degree of insolence and contempt of the authority of the church. And little or nothing could be done further in the affair.

This was the occasion of weakening Mr. Edwards' hands in the work of the ministry, especially among the young people; with whom, by this means, he greatly lost his influence! This seemed in a great measure to put an end to Mr. Edward's usefulness at Northampton, and doubtless laid a foundation, and will help to account for the surprising events which will by and by be related. To be sure he had not great visible success after this; but the influences of God's Spirit were greatly withheld, and security and carnality much increased among them. That great and singular degree of visible religion and good order which had been found among them soon began gradually to decay, and the youth have since been more wanton and dissolute.

Mr. Stoddard, Mr. Edwards' grandfather and predecessor in the work of the ministry, was of the opinion that unconverted persons had a right in the sight of God or considered as such, to the sacrament of the Lord's Supper;[§] that, therefore, it was their duty to come to that ordinance, though they knew they had no true goodness or gospel holiness. He maintained that visible Christianity does not consist in a profession or appearance of that wherein true holiness or real Christianity consists; that, therefore, the profession which persons make in order to be received as visible members of Christ's church ought not to be such as to express or imply a real compliance with or consent to the terms of the covenant of grace or a hearty embracing (of) the gospel. So that they who really reject Jesus Christ, and dislike the gospel-way of salvation in their hearts, and know that this is true of themselves may make the profession without lying and hypocrisy. Accordingly, he endeavored to form a short profession for persons to make in order to be admitted into the church, and come to the sacrament, answerable to this principle; and it took place and was practiced in Northampton; and persons were admitted into the church, and to the sacrament, not under the notion of their being true saints or that they had any real goodness.

Mr. Stoddard's appearing to maintain this principle made a great noise in the country; and he was opposed as introducing something contrary to the principles and practice of almost all the churches in New England. And the matter was publicly controverted between him and Dr. Increase Mather of Boston. However, through Mr. Stoddard's great influence and ascendance over the people at Northampton, it was introduced there though not without opposition. And his principles, by degrees spread very

---

[§] This was also known as the Half-Way Covenant. Solomon Stoddard as minister in Northampton proposed in 1707 to permit or admit the unregenerate to the Lord's Table as a means of grace. This meant that the doctrine of total depravity or inability broke down the new birth in relation to the local church. Mr. Stoddard was instrumental in instituting this practice into regular practice. HRR

much among ministers and people in that country, and in other parts of New England; though no church, except Northampton, publicly and professedly acted upon this principle, by altering the profession that those made who were admitted to the sacrament, to suit it to such a notion; but required of all who joined the church a profession of that wherein true Christianity or real godliness consists. And of late years his opinion, that persons who have no real goodness but are in a Christless state, and know themselves to be so may make a Christian profession, and come to the sacrament without lying and hypocrisy; and that they have a right, and it is their duty to do so, has greatly spread in the country.

Mr. Edwards had some hesitation about this matter when he first settled at Northampton, and afterwards; but did not receive such a degree of conviction that the admitting of persons into the church, who made no pretense to real godliness was wrong, as to prevent his practicing upon it with a good conscience, for some years. But at length his doubts about the matter greatly increased, which put him upon examining it more thoroughly than he had ever before done, by searching the Scripture and reading and examining such books as were written to defend the admission of persons to sacraments without a profession of saving faith. And the result was a full conviction that it was wrong, and that he could not practice ... it with good conscience. He was fully convinced that to be a *visible Christian* was to put on the visibility or appearance of a real Christian; that the profession of Christianity was a profession of that wherein real Christianity consists, was therefore a profession of true respect of Christ, and a hearty embracing the gospel, etc. That therefore no person who rejected Christ in his heart could make such a profession consistent with truth. And, therefore, as the ordinance of the Lord's Supper was instituted for none but visible professing Christians, none but those who are real Christians, have a real right in the sight of God to come to that ordinance; and that none ought to be admitted thereto, who do not make a profession of real Christianity, and so cannot be received in a judgment of charity as true friends to Jesus Christ or real saints.*

When Mr. Edwards' sentiments were known in the spring of the year 1744, it gave great offense, and the town was put into a great ferment; and before he was heard in his own defense or it was known by many what his principles were, the general cry was to have him dismissed as what alone would satisfy them. This was evident from the whole tenor of their conduct, and they neglected and opposed the most proper means of calmly considering, and so understanding the matter in dispute; and persisted in a refusal to attend to what Mr. Edwards had to say in defense of his principles. And, from the beginning to (the) end, opposed the measures which had the best tendency to compromise and heal the difficulty; and with much zeal pursued those which were calculated to make a separation certain and speedy.

Mr. Edwards thought of preaching on the subject, that they might know what were his sentiments, and what were the grounds of them (of both which he was sensible, the most of them were quite ignorant), before they took any step for a separation between him and his people. But that he might do nothing to increase the tumult, but on the contrary take all those steps, which he could with a good conscience that tended to peace, he first proposed the thing to the church's Standing Committee; supposing that if he entered on the subject publicly with their consent it would

---

* They who have a desire more fully to understand this controversy, and know if it is justly represented here, may do it by reading what Mr. Edwards wrote on this occasion in order to explain and vindicate his principles; together with the Rev. Mr. Williams' answer and Mr. Edwards' reply to him. And if they please, they may consult what Dr. Mather and Mr. Stoddard wrote before on this subject.

prevent the ill consequences which otherwise he feared would follow. But the most of them would by no means consent to it, but strenuously opposed it. Upon which he gave it over for the present, as what in such circumstances would rather raise a tumult, and blow the fire up to a greater height than answer the good ends proposed.

Mr. Edwards being sensible that his principles were not understood, and much misrepresented through the country; and finding that his people were in too much of a heat calmly to attend to the matter in controversy then, and were in a disposition even to refuse to hear him preach upon it proposed to print what he had to say on the point, as this seemed to be the only way left him to have a fair hearing. Accordingly his people consented to put off the calling (of) a council, till what he should write was published. But they manifested great uneasiness in waiting before it came out of the press. And when it was published it was read but by very few of them. Mr. Edwards, being sensible of this, renewed his proposal to preach upon it; and, at a meeting of the brethren of the church, asked their consent in the following terms:

I desire that the brethren would manifest their consent, that I should declare the reasons of my opinion relating to full communion in the church, in lectures appointed for that end: not as an act of authority, or as putting the power of declaring the whole counsel of God out of my hands, but for peace sake, and to prevent occasion of strife.

But it passed in the negative.

Mr. Edwards then proposed that it should be left to a few of the neighboring ministers, whether it was not, all things considered, reasonable that he should be heard in this matter from the pulpit, before the affair should be brought to an issue. But this also passed in the negative.

However, he having had the advice of the ministers and messengers of the neighboring churches, who met at Northampton to advise them under their difficulties, proceeded to appoint a lecture in order to preach on the subject, proposing to do so weekly till he had finished what he had to say. On Monday there was a precinct or society meeting in which a vote was passed to choose a committee to go to Mr. Edwards, and desire him not to preach lectures on the subject in controversy, according to his declaration and appointment. And accordingly proceeded to choose a committee of three men for this purpose, who waited on him and did their errand. However, Mr. Edwards thought proper to proceed according to his proposal; and accordingly preached a number of sermons till he had finished what he had to say on the subject. These lectures were very thinly attended by his own people; but great numbers of strangers from the neighboring towns attended them, so many as to make above half the congregation. This was in February and March 1750.

The calling (of) a decisive council to determine the matter of difference between pastor and people; or rather to dismiss the pastor from his church and people (for the delay of which a great deal of impatience had been publicly manifested) was now more particularly attended to by Mr. Edwards and the church.

Mr. Edwards had before this insisted upon it, from time to time, that they were by no means ripe for such a procedure (as they had not yet given him a fair hearing in defense of his cause; which, if they would do, perhaps the need of such a council would be superseded). And besides, he thought there was abundant public evidence that they were not yet in a temper suited to attend on, and be active in, such a transaction as the dissolving of the relation between them and their pastor; which would, as things then stood, probably be the event. He observed,

96

That it was exceedingly unbecoming churches of the Lamb of God to manage their religious affairs of greatest importance in a ferment and tumult, deep humiliation and submission to the awful frowns of heaven, humble dependence on God, and with fervent prayer and supplication to him. That therefore for them to go about such an affair, in such a manner as they did, would be most unbecoming the gospel, greatly to the dishonor of God and religion, and a way in which a people cannot expect a blessing. That such a great affair as this should be gone about with calm consideration; but that such a temper as the people were then in was wholly inconsistent with this.

But having used all the means which he could think of within his power to bring them to a more calm and charitable temper, and to hear and weigh what he had to say in his own defense, with attention and candor; and finding that nothing prevailed, but rather the tumult and uproar was increased, he consented that a decisive council should be called without any further delay.

But a difficulty attended the choice of a council, which was for some time insuperable. It was agreed that the council should be mutually chosen, one half by the pastor and the other half by the church; but the people insisted upon it that he should be confined to the county in his choice. Mr. Edwards thought this an unreasonable restraint on him as it was known that the ministers and churches in that county were almost universally against him in the controversy that divided him and his people, and made the two parties. He indeed did not suppose that the business of the proposed council would be to determine whether his opinion, which was the occasion of the difficulty between him and his people was right or not; or that what they were to judge of depended upon this. But their business would be—to see and determine whether any possible way could be devised for an accommodation between a pastor and people, and to use their wisdom and endeavor in order to this. And if they found this impracticable, they must determine whether things were now ripe for a separation; whether what ought in justice to be previous to a separation had already actually been done, so that there was nothing further in justice to be demanded by either of the parties concerned, before a separation should take place. And if he was dismissed by them it would be their business to set forth to the world in what manner and for what cause he was dismissed; how far he was innocent, and whether he might yet be employed in the work of the ministry, etc. All which were matters of great importance to him, and required upright and impartial judges. And considering the great influence a difference in religious opinions has to prejudice men one against another, and the close connection of the point in which most of the ministers and churches in the county differed from him, with the matter to be judged of, he did not think they could be reasonably looked upon as impartial judges, as that the matter ought to be wholly left to them. Besides, he thought the case being so new and extraordinary required the ablest judges in the land. For these and some other reasons, which he offered, he insisted upon liberty to go out of the county for those members of the proposed council in which he was to have a choice. In this, as was just now said, the people strenuously and obstinately opposed him. They at length agreed to leave the matter to a council consisting of the ministers and messengers of the five neighboring churches; who, after they had met twice upon it, and had the case largely debated before them, were equally divided, and therefore left the matter undetermined.

However, they were all agreed that Mr. Edwards ought to have liberty to go out of the county for *some* of the council. And at the next church meeting, which was on the 26th of March, Mr. Edwards offered to join with them in calling a council if they would consent that he should choose *two* of the churches out of the county, in case the council consisted of but *ten* churches. The church however refused to comply with this at one meeting after another repeatedly; and proceeded to warn a church meeting and choose a moderator, in order to act without their pastor.

But, to pass by many particulars, at length at a meeting of the church, warned by their pastor, May 3, they voted their consent to his proposal of going out of the county for two of the churches that should be applied to. And then they proceeded to make choice of the ten ministers and churches of which the council should consist. Accordingly the churches were sent to, and the council convened on the 19th of June. Who, after they had made some fruitless attempts for a composition between the pastor and church, passed a resolve by the majority of one voice* only, to the following purpose: "That it is expedient that the pastoral relation between Mr. Edwards and his church be immediately dissolved, if the people still persist in desiring it." And it being publicly put to the people, whether they still insisted on Mr. Edwards' dismission from the pastoral office over them? A great majority (above two hundred against twenty), zealously voted for his dismission. And he was accordingly dismissed June 22, 1750.

The dissenting part of the council entered their protest against this proceeding, judging that it was too much in a hurry, as they were by no means ripe for a separation, considering the past conduct and present temper of the people. And some of that part of the council that were active, expressed themselves surprised at the uncommon

---

* One of the churches which Mr. Edwards chose did not see fit to join the council. However, the minister of that church being at Northampton, at the sitting of the council, was desired by Mr. Edwards and the church to sit in council and act, which he did. But there being no messenger from the church, the council was not full, and there was a disparity; by which means doubtless, there was one vote more for an immediate dismission, than against it.

zeal and engagedness of spirit publicly manifested by the people in their voting for a dismission: which evidenced to them, and all observing spectators that they were far from a temper of mind becoming such a solemn and awful transaction, considered in all its circumstances.

Being thus dismissed he preached his farewell sermon on the first of July from 2 Corinthians 1:14. The doctrine he observed from the words was this, "Ministers and the people that have been under their care, must meet one another before Christ's tribunal at the day of judgment." It was a remarkably solemn and affecting discourse, and was published at the desire of some of the hearers.

After Mr. Edwards was dismissed from Northampton he preached there sometimes occasionally, when they had no other preacher to supply the pulpit; till at length a great uneasiness was manifested by many of the people at his preaching there at all. Upon which the committee for supplying the pulpit called the town together to know their minds with respect to that matter; when they voted that it was not agreeable to their minds that he should preach among them. Accordingly, when Mr. Edwards was in town, and they had no other minister to preach to them they carried on public worship among themselves, and without any preaching, rather than to invite Mr. Edwards!

Every one must be sensible that this was a great trial to Mr. Edwards. He had been near twenty-four years among that people; and his labors had been, to all appearance, from time to time greatly blessed among them; and a great number looked on him as their spiritual father, who had been the happy instrument of turning them from darkness to light, and plucking them as brands out of the burning. And they had from time to time professed that they looked upon it as one of their greatest privileges to have such a minister, and manifested their great love and esteem of him, to such a degree that (as St. Paul says of the Galatians), if it had been possible, they would have plucked out their own eyes, and given them to him. And they had a great interest in *his* heart: he had borne them on his heart and carried them in his bosom for many years; exercising a tender concern and love for them: for their good he was always writing, contriving, laboring; for them he had poured out ten thousand fervent prayers; in their good he had rejoiced as one that finds great spoil; and they were dear to him above any other people under heaven.

Now to have *this people* turn against him, and thrust him out from among them in a great tumult and heat, with haste and a great decree of violence; like the Jews of old, stopping their ears and running upon him with furious zeal, not allowing him to defend himself by giving him a fair hearing; and ever refusing so much as to hear him preach; many of them surmising and publicly speaking many ill things as to his ends and designs! To have the tables turned so suddenly, and the voice so general and loud against him. This surely must come very near to him, and try his spirit. The words of the Psalmist seem applicable to this case:

It was not an enemy that reproached me, then I could have borne it; neither was it he that hated me, that did magnify himself against me, then I would have hid myself from him. But it was THOU—my guide and mine acquaintance. We took sweet counsel together, and walked unto the house of God in company.[§]

Let us therefore now *behold the man*!

The calm and sedateness of his mind; his meekness and humility in great and violent opposition, and injurious treatment; his resolution and steady conduct through all this dark and terrible storm were truly wonderful, and cannot be set in so beautiful and affecting a light by any description, as they appeared in to his friends, who were eye witnesses.

Mr. Edwards had a numerous and chargeable family, and little or no income, exclusive of his salary; and

---

[§] Psalm 55:12-14

considering how far he was advanced in years; the general
disposition of people, who want a minister to prefer a young
man who has never been settled to one who has been
dismissed from his people; and what misrepresentations
were made of his principles through the country, it looked
to him not at all probable that he should ever have
opportunity to be settled again in the work of the ministry, if
he was dismissed from Northampton; and he was not
inclined or able to take any other course or go into any other
business to get a living; so that beggary as well as disgrace
stared him full in the face if he persisted in his principles.
To be sure, he viewed himself as taking the most direct way
to these, according to the natural course of things, by
discovering and adhering to his principles in the situation he
then was. For he foresaw all this, before it came upon him;
and therefore had the opportunity and the temptation to
escape it by concealing his principles. When he was fixed
in his principles, and before they were publicly known, he
told some of his friends that if he discovered and persisted
in them it would most likely issue in his dismission and
disgrace, and the ruin of himself and family, as to their
temporal interests. He therefore first sat down and counted
the cost, and deliberately took up the cross, when it was set
before him in its full weight and magnitude, and in direct
opposition to all worldly views and motives. And therefore
his conduct in these circumstances was a remarkable
exercise and discovery of his conscientiousness, and his
readiness to deny himself, and forsake all that he had to
follow Christ.

A man must have a considerable degree of the spirit of
a martyr, not to flinch in such a case as this, but go on with
the steadfastness and resolution with which he did. He, as it
were, put his life in his hand, and ventured on where truth
and duty appeared to lead him, unmoved at the threatening
dangers on every side.

However, God did not forsake him. As he gave him
those inward supports by which he was able in patience to

possess his soul, and calmly and courageously row on in the storm, as it were in the face of boisterous winds, beating hard upon him, and in the midst of gaping waves threatening to swallow him up; so he soon appeared for him, in his providence, even beyond all his expectations. His correspondents and other friends in Scotland hearing of his dismission, and fearing it might be the means of bringing him into worldly straits generously contributed a handsome sum, and sent it over to him.

And God did not leave him without tender, valuable friends at Northampton; for a small number of his people who opposed his dismission from the beginning, and some who acted on neither side, who joined with him after his dismission, and adhered to him under the influence of their great esteem and love of Mr. Edwards, were willing and thought themselves able to maintain him; and insisted upon it, that it was his duty to stay among them as a distinct and separate congregation from the body of the town, who had rejected him.

Mr. Edwards could not see it to be his duty to stay among them as circumstances were, as this would probably be a means of perpetuating an unhappy division in the town; and there was to him no prospect of doing the good there, which would counterbalance the evil. However, that he might do all he could to satisfy his tender and afflicted friends; and because in the multitude of counselors there is safety, he consented to ask the advice of an ecclesiastical council. Accordingly a council was called and convened at Northampton on the 15th of May 1751.

The town on this occasion was put into a great tumult and fire. They, who were active in Mr. Edwards' dismission supposed, though without any ground and contrary to truth, that he was contriving and attempting with his friends, again to introduce himself at Northampton. They drew up a remonstrance against their proceedings, and laid it before the council (though they would not acknowledge them to be an ecclesiastical council), containing many heavy, though groundless insinuations and charges against Mr. Edwards, and bitter accusations of the party who had adhered to him; but refused to appear and support any of their charges or so much as to give the gentlemen of the council any opportunity to confer with them about the affair pending, though it was diligently sought.

The council having heard what Mr. Edwards, and they who adhered to him, and any others who desired to be heard had to say, advised agreeable to Mr. Edwards' judgment and expectation that he should leave Northampton, and accept of the mission to which he was invited at Stockbridge, of which a more particular account will be given presently.

Many other facts relative to this sorrowful, strange, surprising affair (the most so doubtless of any of the kind that ever happened in New England; and, perhaps, in any part of the Christian world), might be related; but as this more general history of it may be sufficient to answer the ends proposed, viz. to rectify some gross misrepresentations that have been made of the matter, and discover the great trial Mr. Edwards had herein, it is thought best to suppress other particulars. As a proper close to this melancholy story, and to confirm and further illustrate what has been related, the following letter from Joseph Hawley, Esq.[§] (a

---

[§] Joseph Hawley was Edwards' cousin whom he described as "a young gentleman of liberal education and notable abilities and a fluent speaker, who was high in their esteem and is become the most leading man in the town." Hawley was a lawyer of some ability, who refused to take a case if his client was known to be dishonest. He has also been described as "one of the younger men in the community for whom the incipient social and religious liberalism of the day had an appeal" [Arthur Cushman McGiffert, Jr., *Jonathan Edwards*, 128]. The question is, "Why would Hawley become the leader of the opposition to oust his cousin Jonathan Edwards from his pastorate?" There has been an ongoing discussion among scholars as to the motive of Hawley without resolve. There is a family history perhaps that should be discussed to some degree.   Solomon Stoddard, Edwards' grandfather, who was a dominating personality in the Connecticut Valley, and through the marriages of his children and stepchildren became the center of an intricate web of family relationships. Stoddard had a daughter Rebecca who married Joseph Hawley, the leading merchant and Justice of the Peace of Northampton. They had a son who was named Joseph; he was twelve when his father died. During the awakening, under Edwards' ministry, in 1735, Joseph Hawley became greatly distraught and was in a melancholic spiritual state; and in this state he committed suicide by cutting his own throat on a Sabbath morning the 1st of June [Harold P. Simonson, *Jonathan Edwards: Theologian of the Heart*, 49; Patricia J. Tracy, *Jonathan Edwards, Pastor*, 116; Perry Miller, *Jonathan Edwards*, 103]. Pastor Edwards believed the devil had precipitated this event which caused the gradual withdrawal of the blessings of the Spirit of God.   Edwards described his uncle as "a gentleman of more than common understanding, of strict morals, religious in his behavior, and a useful honorable person in the town" [Tracy, 116]. Supposedly the Hawley family was excessively prone to melancholy, and it was said to have led to Joseph's mother's death [116]. Edwards stated that Hawley's mental state was tragic but beyond pastoral control [116].   There was also the matter of Joseph Hawley's (who cut his throat in despair of soul) youngest son Elisha. Lieut. Elisha Hawley had been indiscreet with a Martha Root resulting in a child. Edwards led the church to investigate this situation in 1748. Joseph Hawley the brother of Elisha wrote his younger brother, who was on duty at Fort Massachusetts.   The letter informed Elisha that Pastor Edwards was investigating the matter and was pressing for him to marry Martha Root even against her will. Edwards had hoped that his brethren in the ministry would lend support but they did not. Their advice was that Elisha be received back into the church if he made confession of his fornication. Elisha did not marry Martha because of the skillful lawyering of Joseph, who was also in opposition to the pastor's views.   Both Hawley boys had professed Christ under their cousin's ministry, which likely was discomfiting to Edwards [Tracy, 165].   The summer of 1748 was also the matter of disciplining the young people, which led to the removal of

gentleman who was well acquainted with, and very active in the transactions of this whole affair, and very much a head and leader in it), to the Rev. Mr. (David) Hall of Sutton*,

---

Edwards in 1750. The opposition progressed as time elapsed and Joseph Hawley took the lead as chief spokesman for the opposition toward Pastor Edwards [Ola Elizabeth Winslow, *Jonathan Edwards: 1703-1758*, 244 ff.; McGiffert, 128 ff.; Tracy, 185]. What is extraordinary is to read the penitent letter of Joseph Hawley, which was printed in the Boston newspaper. One Edwards scholar noted that Hawley was begging forgiveness for his criminal activity because of fright from Matthew 18:6 [John H. Gerstner, *The Rational Biblical Theology of Jonathan Edwards*, Vol. III, 402]. HRR

* The Rev. Dr. David Hall was born the 6th of August 1704 at Yarmouth, Barnstable, Massachusetts to Joseph Hall (1663-1736/37) and Hannah Miller Hall (1666-1710). He graduated from Harvard College in 1724 and received an honorary degree of D.D. from Dartmouth College in 1777. He was invited to preach at Sutton, Mass. in 1728, and was called to that church and ordained the 15th of October 1729; and he continued in that pastorate till his death almost sixty years later (May 8, 1789). While pastoring in Sutton he met and married Elizabeth Prescott on the 24th of June 1731. Two children were born to this union: Sarah and Lucy Hall. Although David Hall received many calls to more prominent places he remained in Sutton where he was loved and honored. There was a mutual attachment between pastor and people. He was an intimate friend and admirer of Jonathan Edwards. They were united in standing up for what they saw as true revival against many that opposed the notion of revival. They also jointly opposed the excesses that arose to corrupt the revivals. When Edwards was chosen president of Princeton College, David Hall was also being considered for that position [Ellery Bicknell Crane, *Historic Homes and Institutions and Genealogical and Personal Memoirs of Worcester County Massachusetts*, 108]. Little wonder that Edwards wanted his friend to be a participant in the council convened on June 19, 1750 for Jonathan Edwards. Hall in his *Diary* explained how his friend received the expulsion. His entry read: "that faithful Witness received ... Shock, unshaken: I never saw ... (the) lest Symptoms of displeasure in his Countenance the whole week, but

published in a weekly newspaper in Boston, May 19, 1760, is here inserted.

~~~~~~~~
========

To the Rev. Mr. David Hall of Sutton
Northampton, May 9, 1760

Rev. SIR,

I have often wished that every member of the two ecclesiastical councils (that formerly sat in Northampton upon the unhappy differences between our former most worthy and Rev. Pastor Mr. Jonathan Edwards and the church here), whereof you were a member; I say, sir, I have often wished every one of them truly knew my real sense of my own conduct in the affairs that the one and the other of said councils are privy to, myself before God for what was unchristian and sinful in my conduct before said councils, but also to confess my faults to them, and take shame to myself therefore before them. I have often studied with myself in what manner it was practicable for me to do it; and when I understood that you, Sir, and Mr. Eaton were to be at Cold Spring at the time of the late council, I resolved to improve the opportunity fully to open my mind there to you and him thereon; and thought that probably some

---

he appeared like a man of God, whose Happiness was out of ... reach of his Enemies, and whose treasure was not only a future but a present good: overbalancing all Imaginable ills of Life, even to the Astonishment of many, who could not be at rest without his Dismission: it manifestly appeared to me" [Winslow, 236]. Hawley confessed his sin against Pastor Edwards. When? Four years later it was made by Joseph Hawley in a letter to Edwards, and later in a letter to Rev. David Hall as one supporting the minority, which means Edwards. This second letter of Hawley was printed in a Boston newspaper in 1760, after the death of Edwards, and at the request of Hawley [Winslow, 235]. Hawley was truly repentant of his sinful acts. HRR

method might be then thought of, in which my reflections on myself touching the matters, above hinted at, might be communicated to most if not all the gentlemen aforesaid, who did not reside in this county; but you know, Sir, how difficult it was for us to converse together by ourselves when at Cold Spring, without giving umbrage to that people; I therefore proposed writing to you upon the matters which I had then opportunity only just summarily to suggest; which you, Sir, signified would be agreeable to you; I therefore now undertake what I then proposed, in which I humbly ask the Divine aid; and that I may be made most freely willing fully to confess my sin and guilt to you and the world, in those instances which I have reason to suppose fell under your notice, as they were public and notorious transactions, and on account whereof, therefore, you, Sir, and all others who had knowledge thereof, had just cause to be offended at me.

And, in the first place, Sir, I apprehend that, with the church and people of Northampton, I sinned and erred exceedingly in consenting and laboring that there should be so early a dismission of Mr. Edwards from his pastoral relation to us, even upon the supposition that he was really in a mistake in the disputed point: not only because the dispute was upon matters so very disputable in themselves, and at the greatest removal from fundamental, but because Mr. Edwards so long had approved himself a most faithful and painful pastor to said church; and also changed his sentiments in that point wholly from a tender regard to what appeared to him to be truth; and had made known his sentiments with great moderation and upon great deliberation, against all worldly motives, and from mere fidelity to his great Master, and a tender regard to the souls of his flock as we had the highest reason to judge; which considerations now seem to me sufficient; and would (if we had been of a right spirit), have greatly endeared him to his people, and made us to the last degree reluctant to parting with him, and disposed us to the exercise of the greatest candor, gentleness and moderation; how much of the reverse whereof appeared in us I need not tell you, Sir, who was an eyewitness of our temper and conduct.

And, although it does not become me to pronounce decisively, on a point so disputable, as was then in dispute; yet I beg leave to say, that I really apprehend, that it is of the highest moment to the body of this church, and to me in particular, most solicitously to inquire, whether, like the Pharisees and lawyers in John Baptist's time, we did not reject the counsel of God against ourselves, in rejecting Mr. Edwards and his doctrine, which was the ground of his dismission. And I humbly conceive, that it highly imports us all of this church, most seriously and impartially to examine what that most worthy and able divine published, about that time, in support of the same, whereby he being dead yet speaketh.

But there were three things, Sir, especially, in my own particular conduct before the first council, which have been justly matter of great grief and much trouble to me, almost ever since; *vis.*

In the first place, I confess, Sir, that I acted very immodestly and abusively to you, as well as injuriously to the church and myself, when with much zeal and unbecoming assurance, I moved the council that they would interpose to silence and stop you, in an address you were making one morning to the people, wherein you were, if I do not forget, briefly exhorting them to a tender remembrance of the former affection and harmony, that had long subsisted between them and their reverend pastor, and the great comfort and profit which they apprehended that they had received from his ministry; for which, Sir, I heartily ask your forgiveness; and I think, that we ought, instead of opposing an exhortation of that nature, to have received it with all thankfulness.

Another particular of my conduct before that council, which I now apprehend was criminal, and was owing to the want of that tender affection, and reverend respect and esteem for Mr. Edwards, which he had highly merited of me, was my strenuously opposing the adjournment of the matters submitted to that council for about two months; for which I declare myself unfeignedly sorry; and I with shame remember, that I did it in a peremptory, decisive, vehement and very immodest manner.

But, Sir, the most criminal part of my conduct at that time, that I am conscious of, was my exhibiting to that council a set of arguments in writing, the drift whereof was to prove the reasonableness and necessity of Mr. Edwards' dismission, in case no accommodation was then effected with mutual consent; which writing, by clear implication, contained some severe, uncharitable, and, if I remember right, groundless and slanderous imputations on Mr. Edwards, expressed in bitter language; and although the original draft thereof was not done by me, yet I foolishly and sinfully consented to copy it; and, as agent for the church, to read it, and deliver it to the council, which I could never have done, if I had not had a wicked relish for perverse things, which conduct of mine I confess was very sinful, and highly provoking to God; for which I am ashamed, confounded, and have nothing to answer.

As to the church's remonstrance (as it was called), which their committee preferred to the last of the said councils, to all which I was consenting, and in the composing whereof I was very active, as also in bringing the church to their vote upon it; I would, in the first place, only observe that I do not remember any thing, in that small part of it, which was plainly discursive of the expediency of Mr. Edwards' resettlement here, as pastor to a part of the church, which was very exceptionable; but as to all the residue, which was much the greatest part thereof (and I am not certain that any part was wholly free), it was every where interlarded with unchristian bitterness, sarcastical and unmannerly insinuations, contained divers direct, grievous, and criminal charges and allegations against Mr. Edwards, which, I have since good reason to suppose, were all founded on jealous and uncharitable mistakes, and so were really gross slanders; also many heavy and reproachful charges upon divers of Mr. Edwards' adherents, and some severe censures of them all indiscriminately; all of which (if not wholly false and groundless), were altogether unnecessary, and therefore highly criminal. Indeed, I am fully convinced that the whole of that composure, excepting the small part thereof above mentioned, was totally unchristian a scandalous, abusive, injurious, libel against Mr. Edwards and his particular friends; especially the former, and highly provoking and detestable in the sight of God, for which I am heartily sorry and ashamed; and pray that I may re-member it with deep abasement and penitence all my days. Nor do I now think that the church's conduct in refusing to appear and attend before that council, to support the charges and allegations in the said remonstrance against Mr. Edwards and the said brethren, which they demanded, was ever vindicated by all the subtle answers that were given to the said demand; nor do I think that our conduct in that instance was capable of a defense; for it appears to me that by making such charges against them before the said council, we necessarily so far gave that council jurisdiction; and I own with sorrow and regret that I zealously endeavored, that the church should perseveringly refuse to appear before the said council, for the purpose aforesaid, which I humbly pray God to forgive.

Another part of my conduct Sir, of which I have long repented, and for which I hereby declare my hearty sorrow, was my obstinate opposition to the last council's having any conference with the church; which the said council earnestly and repeatedly moved for, and which the church (as you know), finally denied. I think it discovered a great deal of pride and vain sufficiency in the church, and showed them to be a very opinionative, especially the chief sticklers, one of whom, I own, I was; and think it was running a most presumptuous risk, and acting the part of proud scorners for us to refuse hearing, and candidly and seriously considering

111

what that council could say or oppose to us; among whom, there were divers justly in great reputation for grace and wisdom.

In these instances, Sir, of my conduct, and in others (to which you were not privy), in the course of that most melancholy contention with Mr. Edwards, I now see that I was very much influenced by vast pride, self-sufficiency, ambition and vanity. I appear to myself vile and doubtless much more so to others, who are more impartial; and do, in the review thereof, abhor myself, and repent sorely: and if my own heart condemns me, it behooves me solemnly to remember that God is greater and knows all things; and I hereby own, Sir, that such treatment of Mr. Edwards, as is herein before mentioned, wherein I was so deeply concerned and active, was particularly and very aggravatedly sinful and ungrateful in me, because I was not only under the common obligations of each individual of the society to him, as to a most able, diligent, and faithful pastor; but I had also received many instances of his tenderness, goodness and generosity to me as a young kinsman, whom he was disposed to treat in a most friendly manner.

Indeed, Sir, I must own that by my conduct in consulting and acting against Mr. Edwards within the time of our most unhappy disputes with him, and especially in and about that abominable remonstrance, I have so far symbolized with Balaam, Ahitophel, and Judas that I am confounded and filled with terror oftentimes when I attend to the most painful similitude.

And I freely confess, that, on account of my conduct above mentioned, I have the greatest reason to tremble at those most solemn and awful words of our Saviour, Matt. 18:6, and those of Luke 17 at the 2nd verse: "Whoso shall offend one of these little ones, which believe in me, it were better for him that a millstone were hanged about his neck, and that he were drowned in the depth of the sea," and those in Luke 10:16, "He that despiseth you, despiseth me: and he that despiseth me, despiseth him that sent me," and I am most sorely sensible that nothing but that infinite grace and mercy which saved some of the betrayers and murderers of our blessed Lord, and the persecutors of his martyrs, can pardon me; in which alone I hope for pardon, for the sake of Christ, whose blood (blessed be God), cleanses from all sin. On the whole, Sir, I am convinced that I have the greatest reason to say as David, "Have mercy upon me, O God, according to thy loving-kindness, according to the multitude of thy tender mercies, blot out my transgressions; wash me thoroughly from mine iniquity, and cleanse me from my sin: for I acknowledge my transgressions, and my sin is ever before me.... Hide thy face from my sins, and blot out all mine iniquities; create in me a clean heart, O God, and renew a right spirit within me; cast me not away from thy presence, and take not thy Holy Spirit from me, restore unto me the joy of thy salvation, and uphold me with thy free Spirit" (Ps. 51:1-3, 9-12).

And I humbly apprehend that it greatly concerns the church of Northampton most seriously to examine, whether the many hard speeches, spoken by many particular members, against their former pastor, some of which the church really countenanced, and especially those spoken by the church as a body, in that most vile remonstrance, are not so odious and ungodly, as to be utterly incapable of defense; and whether the said church were not guilty of a great sin in being so willing and disposed, for so slight a cause, to part with so faithful and godly a minister as Mr. Edwards was. And whether ever God will hold us guiltless till we cry to him for Christ's sake, to pardon and save us from that judgment, which such ungodly deeds deserve, and publicly humble and take shame to ourselves there for. And I most heartily wish and pray that the town and church of Northampton would seriously and carefully examine whether they have not abundant cause to judge that they are now lying under great guilt in the sight of God; and whether those of us, who were concerned in that most awful contention with Mr. Edwards, can ever more reasonably expect God's favor and blessing, till our eyes are opened, and we become thoroughly convinced that we have greatly provoked the Most High, and have been injurious to one of the best of men; and until we shall be thoroughly convinced that we have dreadfully persecuted Christ by persecuting and vexing that just man and servant of Christ; until we shall be humble as in the dust on account of it, and till we openly, in full terms, and without baulking the matter, confess the same before the world, and most humbly and earnestly seek forgiveness of God, and do what we can to honor the memory of Mr. Edwards, and clear it of all the aspersions which we unjustly cast upon him, since God has been pleased to put it beyond our power to ask his forgiveness. Such terms, I am persuaded, the great and righteous God will hold us to, and that it will be vain for us to hope to escape with impunity in any other way. This I am convinced of with regard to myself, and this way I most solemnly propose to take myself (if God in his mercy shall give me opportunity), that so, by making free confession to God and man of my sin and guilt, and publicly taking shame to myself there for, I may give glory to the God of Israel, and do what in me lies to clear the memory of that venerable man from the wrongs and injuries I was so active in bringing on his reputation and character; and I thank God that he has been pleased to spare my life and opportunity there for to this time, and am sorry that I have delayed the affair so long.

Although I made the substance of almost all the foregoing reflections in writing, but not exactly in the same manner, to Mr. Edwards and the brethren who adhered to him, in Mr. Edwards' life, and before he removed from Stockbridge, and I have reason to believe that he, from his great candor and charity, heartily forgave me and prayed for me; yet, because that was not generally known, I look on myself obliged to take further steps; for *while I kept silence my bones waxed old,* etc.

For all these my great sins, therefore, in the first place, I humbly and most earnestly ask forgiveness of God; in the next place, of the relatives and near friends of Mr. Edwards. I also ask the forgiveness of all those who were called Mr. Edwards' adherents; and of all the members of the ecclesiastical councils above mentioned; and lastly, of all Christian people, who have had any knowledge of the matters above said or any of them.

I have no desire, Sir, that you should make any secret of this letter; but desire you would communicate the same to whom you shall judge proper; and I purpose (if God shall give me opportunity) to procure it to be published in some one of the public newspapers; for I cannot devise any other way of making known my sentiments of the foregoing matters to all who ought to be acquainted therewith, and therefore I think I ought to do it, whatever remarks I may foresee will be made thereon.

Probably when it comes out, some of my acquaintance will pronounce me quite over-run with vapors; others will be furnished with matter for mirth and pleasantry; others will cursorily pass it over, as relating to matters quite stale; but some I am persuaded, will rejoice to see me brought to a sense of my sin and duty; and I myself shall be conscious that I have done something of what the nature of the case admits, towards undoing what is, and long has been, to my greatest remorse and trouble, that it was ever done.

Sir, I desire that none would entertain a thought from my having spoken respectfully of Mr. Edwards, that I am disaffected to our present pastor; for the very reverse is true; and I have a reverend esteem, real value, and hearty affection for him; and bless God that he has, notwithstanding all our former unworthiness, given us one to succeed Mr. Edwards, who (as I have reason to hope) is truly faithful.

I conclude this long letter, by heartily desiring your prayers that my repentance of my sins above mentioned may be unfeigned and genuine, and such as God in infinite mercy, for Christ's sake, will accept; and I beg leave to subscribe myself,

Sir, your real, though very unworthy friend,

and obedient servant,

JOSEPH HAWLEY.

~~~~~~~~~

To Major Joseph Hawley

[What follows is President Jonathan Edwards' letter to Joseph Hawley in reply to his previous personal letter. The previous letter in this book published in Boston by Hawley was a public confession of his wrong doing toward his pastor and relative. The following letter was in answer to a personal letter from Hawley to Edwards dealing with his part in the dismission. Edwards a few weeks before writing this letter had accepted the presidency of the College of New Jersey or Princeton. Hawley Edwards' cousin was in his mid twenties when he took a leading part in the dismission of his pastor. He came under deep conviction of having wronged Pastor Edwards and corresponded with him a number of times. The effect of the following letter upon Hawley was said to have been very powerful. This letter likely led to the previous letter published May 19, 1760. Edwards' death had occurred March 22nd, 1758, which likely added weight to what Hawley wrote in 1760. The following letter was not originally in this volume, but the editor adds it for its historic value to the Sprinkle Publications edition.]

Stockbridge, Nov. 18, 1757

Rev. SIR,

I now, as soon as I am able, set myself about answering your letter of August 11, though I am still so weak that I can write but with a trembling hand, as you may easily perceive. I was taken ill, about the middle of July, and my fits have now left me a little more than a fortnight; but I have been greatly reduced by so long continued an illness, and gain strength very slowly, and cannot be so particular in my answer to your letter, as I might be, if I had more strength.

I rejoice in the good temper and disposition of mind, which seemed to be manifested in your letter; and hope that, whatever I may have suffered, and however greatly I may think myself injured in that affair, which is the subject of your letter, wherein you was so much of a leader, I have a disposition in my consideration of the affair, and what I shall write upon it, to treat you with true candor and Christian charity. Nevertheless, I confess that the thing you desire of me is disagreeable to me, viz., very particularly giving my judgment concerning your conduct in that affair; and it is with no small reluctance that I go about answering such a request, upon two accounts: 1st, as it obliges me renewedly to revolve in my mind, and particularly to look over that most disagreeable and dreadful scene, the particulars of which I have long since very much dismissed from my mind, as having no pleasure in the thought of them. And 2ndly, as it is (and will be looked upon by you, however serious and conscientious you may be in your desires and endeavors to know the truth), a giving a judgment in my own case, a case wherein I was concerned to a very high degree; and therefore will be much more likely to be a giving of it in vain. Notwithstanding, seeing you desire it, and seem to desire it in so Christian a manner, I will give you my judgment plainly, such as it is, and as impartially as I am able, leaving the consequence with God.

You know very well that I looked on myself, in the time of the affair, as very greatly injured by the people in general, in the general conduct, management and progress of it from the beginning to the end. That this was then my judgment was plain enough to be seen; and I suppose, no man in the town was insensible of it. And what were the main things wherein I looked on myself as injured, and what I supposed to be the aggravation of the injury, was also manifested. As particularly that the church and

117

precinct had all imaginable reason to think, that in my receiving that opinion which was the subject of the controversy, and in the steps I took upon it, the declaration I made of it, etc., I acted altogether conscientiously, and from tenderness of spirit, and because I greatly feared to offend God; without, yea, to the highest degree, against all influence of worldly interest, and all private and sinister views. I think it was hardly possible for the affair to be attended with circumstances exhibiting greater evidence of this. I think, if my people therefore, when the affair was first divulged, had been actuated by a Christian spirit or indeed by humanity, (though they might have been very sorry and full of concern about the affair), they would, especially concerning how long I had been their pastor, and they had always from the beginning, and from so long experience, acknowledged me to be their faithful pastor, and most of them esteemed me to be the chief instrument in the hand of God of the eternal salvation of their souls; I say, they would have treated me, if influenced by Christianity and humanity, with the utmost tenderness, calmness and moderation, not to say honor and reverence; and would have thought themselves bound to have gone far in the exercise of patience. But instead of this, the town and church were at once put into the greatest flame: the town was soon filled with talk of dismissing and expelling me, and with contrivances how to do it speedily and effectually. And a most jealous eye from this day forward was kept upon me, lest I should do that slyly and craftily, that should tend to hinder such a design. And almost every step that I took in the affair was by their suspicious eyes looked upon in such a view; and therefore, everything served to renew and heighten the flame of their indignation. Even when I addressed myself to them in the language of moderation and entreaty, it was interpreted as a design to flatter the people, especially the more ignorant to work upon their affections, and so to gain a party, and prevent a vote for my dismission or at least to prevent the people's being united in any full

118

vote. And there was no way that I could lead myself, nothing that I could do or say, but it would have some such uncharitable construction put upon it. As I began the affair in the fear of God, after much and long continued prayer to him, so I was very careful in the whole progress of it, and in every step, to act (undisguisedly) and to avoid any unrighteousness and underhanded measure; nor had I ever once formed a design forever to establish myself at Northampton, and impose myself on the people, whether we should remain differing in our opinion on the point constantly or not; nor did I ever take one step with any such view. The things I aimed at were these two: *1st*, that the people should be brought to a calm temper before extremes were proceeded to; and *2ndly*, that they should, in such a temper, hear what I had to say for myself and my opinion. But nothing could be done. The people most manifestly continued in a constant flame of high resentment and vehement opposition for more than two years together; and this spirit, instead of subsiding, grew higher and higher, till they had obtained their end in my expulsion. Nor indeed did it cease then, but still they maintained their jealousy of me, as if I was fiercely doing the part of an enemy to them, so long as I had a being in the town; yea, till they saw the town well cleared of all my family. So deep was their prejudice that their heat was maintained, nothing would quiet them, till they could see the town clear of root and branch, name and remnant.

I could mention many things that were said and done, in a public manner, in meetings of the precinct, church and their committee, from time to time, from the beginning, fully to justify and support what I have said and supposed, till my dismission, (besides the continual talk in all parts of the town, in private houses, and occasional companies). But I think this cannot be expected; as it would be writing a history that would take up no less than a quire of paper. I would only observe that I was from time to time reprehended by one that was commonly chosen moderator of special and church meetings, and chairman of their committees, in a very dogmatical and magisterial manner, for making so much mischief, putting the church to so much trouble, and once he told me, he did it by the desire and vote of the whole committee, which was very large, consisting of all or most of the chief men of the town. I was often charged with acting only from sinister views, from stiffness of spirit, and from pride, and in arbitrary and tyrannical spirit, and a design, and vast expectation of forcing all to comply with my opinion. The above mentioned persons chiefly approved by the town and church, and set at their head in temporal affairs, once said expressly in a church meeting in the meeting-house, "that it was apparent that I regarded my own temporal interest more than the good of the church; that the church had reason to think I designedly laid a snare to ensnare the church; and that they had best by all means to beware and see to it that they were not ensnared." And he said much more to the same purposed and he was never frowned upon but smiled upon by the church, continuing in such a way of treatment of me, was still made much of, and set foremost in the management of the affair. There were multitudes of precinct and church meetings, many meetings of committees, and conference with me about this affair. I am persuaded there was not one meeting, but that this unreasonable, violent spirit was apparent, and as governing and prevalent. It seemed in the very beginning to govern in all proceedings, and almost every step that was taken. The people were so far from feeling any compassion that it was often declared in the meetings, that if I would retain my opinion, in Mr. Stoddard's way, they would by no means have me for their minister, and their committee declared (here the manuscript is illegible).

It being thus, I think the whole management of the affairs was exceeding provoking and abominable to God; as most contrary to what ought to be in public affairs, especially affairs of religion, and the action of Christian societies; and so contrary to the treatment due to me from that people; and especially in an affair so circumstanced, wherein they had such glaring evidence of my acting only from tenderness of conscience, and with regard to the account I had to give to my great Master, and wherein I so carefully avoided everything irritating, and never offered the people any provocation, unless yielding and condescending as I did to them, (in things which I supposed they insisted on merely from humor and prejudice), in many instances for peace's sake was a provocation; an affair, wherein I with great constancy maintained a diligent watch over my own spirit; an affair, wherein I sought peace and pursued it, and strove to my utmost, to avoid occasions of strife, and to treat every one in a Christian manner.

, Such an affair being so managed, I think no one should have put their hands to it, unless it were to check and restrain, and if possible to bring the people to an exceeding different temper and manner of conduct, and convince and show them how far they were out of the way of their duty. And till this could be done, I think not a step should have been taken by any means to promote and forward their designs. Instead of this, I am persuaded, a judicious Christian, in a right temper of mind, being a bystander would have beheld the scene with horror; especially considering the dreadful work that was making with the credit and interest of religion, by such a town and church as that of Northampton and of such a profession and fame.

And, therefore, Sir, I think you made yourself greatly guilty in the sight of God, in the part you acted in this affair; becoming, especially, towards the latter part of it, very much their leader in it; and much from your own forwardness, putting yourself forward as it were, as though fond of intermeddling and helping, which was the less becoming, considering your youth, and considering your relation to me. Your forwardness especially appeared on this occasion that after you were chosen as one of a committee to plead their cause before a council, you came

121

to me and desired me to stay the church, on purpose that you might have opportunity to excuse yourself from the business, which was accordingly done, and you did excuse yourself, and were excused. But yet when the matter came to be pleaded before the council, you [I think very inconsistently], thrust yourself forward, and pleaded the cause with much earnestness, notwithstanding. 'Tis manifest that what you did in the affair, from time to time, not only helped the people to gain their end in dismissing me, but much encouraged and promoted the spirit with which it was done; your confident, magisterial, vehement manner had a natural and direct tendency to it.

As to your remonstrance to the last council, it not only contained things that were uncharitable and censorious, by which facts were misinterpreted and overstrained, but it was full of direct, bold slanders, asserted in strong terms, and delivered in very severe opprobrious language, merely on suspicion and surmise. As particularly therein, if I mistake not, was asserted that I had said after my dismission, "that I was still *de jure** and *de facto*§ the pastor of that church," which was a false charge. Again, I was charged with having a desire to be settled over a few of the members of the church, to the destruction of the whole; and that I set out once on a journey with a certain gentleman to procure a council to install me at Northampton, and that I contrived to do it at such a time, because I knew that the church was at that time about to send for a candidate, etc., that I might prevent their success therein, and that I was ready to settle in that place, and for the sake of it had refused an invitation to Stockbridge, that I had neglected this opportunity for the sake of settling over an handful. That I had a great inclination to continue at Northampton as a minister, at the expense of the peace and prosperity of the greater part of the town, yea, that I was greatly engaged for it. Here is a

---

* *de jure* of right, legitimate, lawful, by right or just title.
§ *de facto* in fact, in deed, actually.

heap of direct slanders, positively asserted, all contrary to the truth of fact. I had not refused the invitation to Stockbridge or neglected that opportunity. I had no inclination or desire to settle over those few at Northampton, but a very great opposition in my mind to it, abundantly manifested in what I continually said to them, on occasion of their great and constant urgency. It was much more agreeable to my inclination to settle at Stockbridge. And though I complied with the calling of a council to advise in the affair, it was on these terms that it should not be thought hard that I should fully and strongly lay before them all my objections against it. My discourse, with particular ministers in their own houses was chiefly in opposition to Col. D_____t; and so was my discourse before the council when met. I earnestly argued before them, against their advising me to settle there, with hopes that what I said would prevail against it, and very much with that conclusion; and what I said against it was the thing that did prevail against it, and that only. I complied to the calling of the council, and with a view to these two things: first, to quiet the minds of those, who, in so trying a time, had appeared my steadfast friends; that they might not already think exceeding hardly of me; and secondly, the country having been filled with gross misrepresentations of the controversy between me and my people, and the affair of my dismission, and the grounds of it, and the great wounding of my character at a distance, I was willing some ministers of chief note should come from distant parts of the country, and be upon the spot, and see the state of things with their own eyes. It was very contrary to truth, that I contrived to set out at that particular time, because just then the church was about to apply to a candidate, etc., that I might prevent their success; for I knew not of any such thing. I had then no notice of that design or determination of the church. Nor was that true, that is suggested, that the procuring a council was the thing that occasioned our setting out on that journey. Each of us had other business, and should have gone had no such thing as a council been projected; and therefore we went far beyond all parts where any of these ministers dwelt, and spent much more time there than with any of them. As to my seeking to disappoint and ruin the town, and destroy its peace, etc., I did not, in all this affair, take one step with any view at all to a disappointment of the town and church, in any of their measures for settling another minister. I might mention other things in the remonstrance, but I am weary.

These things being so, I cannot think the church's "reflections" do, in any wise, impair their faults in this matter, and the injuries therein done to me. In these "reflections," they grant that they used too strong terms, and language too harsh, that in some things they were too censorious, and had not sufficient grounds to go so far in their charges, that they should not have expressed themselves thus and thus, but had better have used other specified terms, which yet would have been to the hurt of my reputation. I confess, dear Sir, I have no imagination that such sort of reflections and retractions as these will be accepted in the sight of God as sufficient, and all that is proper in such a case; and thus it will be found, that they that think so, do greatly deceive themselves. The church, in their remonstrance seemed to contrive for the strongest, most severe, opprobrious and aggravating kind of terms, to blacken my character, and wound my reputation in the most public manner possible. In their reflections on themselves, a contrary course is taken; there, instead of aggravating their own faults (which is the manner of true penitents), they most manifestly contrive for the softest, mildest terms, to touch their own faults in the most gentle manner possible, by the softest language.

On the whole, Sir, (as you have asked my opinion), I think that that town and church lies under great guilt in the sight of God; and they never more can reasonably expect God's favor and blessing, till they have their eyes opened to be convinced of their great provocation of the Most High, and injuriousness to man, and have their temper greatly altered, till they are deeply humbled, and till they openly and in full terms confess themselves guilty, in the manner in which they are guilty indeed, (and what my opinion of that is, I have in some measure declared), and openly humble and take shame to themselves before the world, and particularly confess their faults and seek forgiveness where they have been peculiarly injurious. Such terms, I am persuaded, the righteous God will hold that people to; and that it will forever be in vain for them to think to go free and escape with impunity in any other way. Palliating and extenuating matters, and daubing themselves over with untempered mortar, and sewing fig-leaves will be in vain before Him whose pure and omniscient eye is as a flame of fire. It has often been observed, what a curse persons have lived under and been pursued by for their ill treatment of their natural parents; but especially may this be expected to follow such abuses offered by a people to one who, in their own esteem is their spiritual father. Expositors and divines often observe that abuse of God's messengers has commonly been the last sin of an offending, backsliding people, which has filled up the measure of their sin, and put an end of God's patience with them, and brought on them ruin. And 'tis also commonly observed that the heads and leaders of such a people have been remarkably distinguished in the fruits of God's vengeance in such cases. And as you, Sir, distinguished yourself as a head and leader to that people in these affairs, at least the main of them; so, I think, the guilt that lies on you in the sight of God is distinguishing, and that you may expect to be distinguished by God's frown, unless there be true repentance, and properly expressed and manifested, with endeavors to be a leader of the people in the affair of repentance, as in their transgression.

One thing which, I think, aggravated your fault, was that you generally thought me in the right in that opinion, wherein I differed from my people. As to the nature and

125

essence of true religion, my people and I, in general, were agreed. The strong point, wherein we differed was that supposing that our common opinion of the nature of true godliness to be right, a profession of it or of those things wherein we supposed the essence of it consisted was necessary to Christian communion. In this, you agreed with me, and not with the people; so that, in effect, you owned my cause or the thing which was the main foundation of the controversy, to be good; and yet in the manner before observed, set yourself as their head in their violent opposition to me. You say that in all your disputes you ever had a full persuasion of my sincerity and true sanctity. If so, then doubtless, what Christ said to his disciples takes hold of you. *He that receiveth you receiveth me, and he that despiseth you despiseth me, and he that despiseth me despiseth him that sent me. And take heed, ye despise not one of these little ones. He that offendeth one of them, it were better for him that a millstone were hanged about his neck, and he drowned in the depths of the sea.*

Thus, Sir, I have done the thing which you requested of me. I wish you may accept it in as Christian a manner as you asked it. You may possibly think that the plain way in which I have given my judgment shows that I am far from being impartial, and that I show a disposition to aggravate and enhance things, and set them forth in the blackest colors, and that I plainly manifest ill will to you. All that I shall say to this is that if you think so, I think you are mistaken. And having performed the disagreeable task you desired of me, I must leave you to judge for yourself concerning what I say. I have spoken my judgment with as great a degree of impartiality as I am master of, and that which is my steady and constant judgment of this awful affair, and I doubt not, will be my judgment as long as I live. One thing I must desire of you, and that is, if you dislike what I have written, you would not expect that I should carry on any farther a letter controversy with you on the subject. I have had enough of this controversy, and desire to have done with it. I have spent enough of the precious time of my life in it heretofore. I desire and pray that God may enable you to view things truly, and as he views them, and so to act in the affair as shall be best for you, and most for your peace, living and dying.

With respectful salutations to your spouse, I am, Sir, your kinsman and friend that sincerely wishes your truest and greatest welfare and happiness in this world and the world to come.

Jonathan Edwards

***

Section III

HIS MISSION TO THE INDIANS AT STOCKBRIDGE, &c.

℮he Indian mission at Stockbridge, (a town in the western part of the province of Massachusetts Bay, sixty miles from Northampton), being vacant by the death of the late Rev. Mr. Sergeant,* the honored and reverend commissioners for Indian affairs in Boston, who have the care and direction of it, applied to him, as the most suitable person they could think of to betrust with the mission. And he was at the same time invited by the inhabitants of Stockbridge; and being advised by the council above mentioned to accept of the invitation, he repaired to Stockbridge, and was introduced and fixed as missionary to the Indians there, by an ecclesiastical council called for that purpose, August 8, 1751.

When Mr. Edwards first engaged in the mission, there was a hopeful prospect of its being extensively serviceable, under his care and influence, not only to that tribe of Indians which was settled at Stockbridge, but among the Six Nations;§ some of whom were coming to Stockbridge to settle, and bring their own, and as many of their neighboring children as they could get to be educated and instructed there. For this end a house for a boarding-school, which was projected by Mr. Sergeant, was erected on a tract of

---

* John Sergeant was the first missionary to the Indians at Stockbridge. The mission to the Indians had originated in Northampton in 1734 at the home of Col. John Stoddard, who was a leader in the town and church. Edwards had been one of the interested parties in originating this mission. Samuel Hopkins had sponsored Edwards to succeed Sergeant in 1751. HRR
§ Mohawks, Oneidas, Onondagas, Cayugas, Senecas aka Iroquois-Huron and Tuscaroras.

land appropriated to that use by the Indians at Stockbridge, where the Indian children, male and female, were to be educated by being clothed and fed, and instructed by proper persons in useful learning. And the boys (were) to be taught husbandry or mechanic trades, and the girls all sorts of women's work. For the encouragement of which, some generous subscriptions were made both in England and America. And the great and general court of the province of Massachusetts Bay did much to promote the affair, and provided lands for the Mohawks to settle on, who should incline to come. And the generous Mr. (Isaac) Hollis, to encourage the thing, ordered twenty-four Indian children to be educated on the same footing, wholly at his cost. Also the society in London for the propagating of the gospel among the Indians in and about New England, directed their commissioners in Boston to do considerable towards this design.

But partly by reason of some unhappy differences that took place among those who had the chief management of this affair at Stockbridge, of which a particular account would not be proper in this place; and partly by the war's breaking out between England and France, which is generally very fatal to such affairs among Indians, this hopeful prospect came to nothing.

Mr. Edwards' labors were attended with no remarkable visible success while at Stockbridge, though he performed the business of his mission to the good acceptance of the inhabitants in general, both English and Indians, and of the commissioners, who supported him honorably, and confided very much in his judgment and wisdom, in all matters relating to the mission.

Stockbridge proved to Mr. Edwards a more quiet, and, on many accounts, a much more comfortable situation than he was in before. It being so much in one corner of the country, his time was not so much taken up with company as it was in Northampton, though many of his friends, from among all parts of the land, often made him pleasant and profitable visits. And he had not so much concern and trouble with other churches as he was obliged to have when at Northampton, by being frequently sought to for advice, and called to assist in ecclesiastical councils. Here, therefore, he followed his beloved study more closely, and to better purpose than ever. In these six years he doubtless made swifter advances in knowledge than ever before, and added more to his manuscripts than in any six years of his life.

And this was probably as useful a part of his life as any; for in this time he wrote the two last books that have been published by him, (of which a more particular account will be given hereafter), by which he has doubtless greatly served the church of Christ, and will be a blessing to many thousands yet unborn.

Thus, after his uprightness and faithfulness had been sufficiently tried at Northampton, his kind Master provided for him a quiet retreat, which was rendered the more sweet by the preceding storm, and where he had a better opportunity to pursue and finish the work God had for him to do.

_____ *** _____

SECTION IV

*HIS BEING MADE PRESIDENT OF NEW JERSEY
COLLEGE; HIS SICKNESS AND DEATH*

On the 24th of September 1757, the Rev. Mr. Aaron
Burr, President of New Jersey College died. And at the
next meeting of the trustees, Mr. Edwards was chosen his
successor; the news of which was quite unexpected, and not
a little surprising to him. He looked on himself, in many
respects, so unqualified for that business that he wondered
that gentlemen of so good judgment, and so well acquainted
with him, as he knew some of the trustees were, should
think of him for that place. He had many objections in his
own mind against understanding the business, both from his
unfitness, and his particular circumstances, yet could not
certainly determine that it was not his duty to accept. The
following extract of a letter, which he wrote to the trustees,
will give the reader a view of his sentiments and exercises
on this occasion, as well as of the great designs he was
deeply engaged in, and zealously prosecuting.

~~~~~~~~~
=========

Stockbridge, 19th Oct. 1757

Rev. and Hon. Gentlemen,

I was not a little surprised on receiving the unexpected
notice of your having made choice of me to succeed the late
President Burr, as the head of Nassau Hall. I am much in
doubt whether I am called to undertake the business, which
you have done me the unmerited honor to choose me for. If
some regard may be had to my outward comfort, I might
mention the many inconveniences and great detriment
which may be sustained, by my removing with my

131

numerous family, so far from all the estate I have in the world, (without any prospect of disposing of it, under present circumstances without losing it in great part), how when we have scarcely got over the trouble and damage sustained by our removal from Northampton, and have but just begun to have our affairs in a comfortable situation for a subsistence in this place; and the experience I must immediately be at to put myself into circumstances tolerably comporting with the needful support of the honor of the office I am invited to, which will not well consist with my ability. But this is not my main objection: the chief difficulties in my mind, in the way of accepting this important and arduous office, are these two: First, my own defects, unfitting me for such an undertaking, many of which are generally known; besides others, which my own heart is conscious to. I have a constitution, in many respects peculiarly unhappy, attended with flaccid solids, vapid, fizzy and scarce fluids, and a low tide of spirits; often occasioning a kind of childish weakness and contemptibleness of speech, presence and demeanor; with a disagreeable dullness and stiffness, much unfitting me for conversation, but more especially for the government of a college. This poorness of constitution makes me shrink at the thoughts of taking upon me, in the decline of life, such a new and great business, attended with such a multiplicity of cares, and requiring such a degree of activity, alertness and spirit of government; especially as succeeding one, so remarkably well qualified in these respects, giving occasion to every one to remark the wide difference. I am also deficient in some parts of learning, particularly in algebra, and the higher parts of mathematics, and in the Greek classics; my Greek learning having been chiefly in the New Testament. The other thing is this: that my engaging in this business will not well consist with those views, and that course of employ in my study, which have long engaged and swallowed up my mind, and been the chief entertainment and delight of my life.

And here, honored Sirs, (emboldened by the testimony I have now received of your unmerited esteem, to rely on your candor), I will with freedom open myself to you.

My method of study, from my first beginning the work of the ministry, has been very much by writing: applying myself in this way to improve every important hint; pursuing the clue to my utmost, when any thing in reading, meditation or conversation has been suggested to my mind, that seemed to promise light in any weighty point. Thus penning what appeared to me my best thoughts, on innumerable subjects for my own benefit. The longer I prosecuted my studies in this method, the more habitual it became, and the more pleasant and profitable I found it. The further I traveled in this way, the more and wider the field opened, which has occasioned my laying out many things, in my mind, to do in this manner, if God should spare my life, which my heart has been much upon: particularly many things against most of the prevailing errors of the present day, which I cannot with any patience see maintained, (to the utter subverting of the gospel of Christ), with so high a hand, and so long continued a triumph with so little control, when it appears so evident to me, that there is truly no foundation for any of this glorying and insult. I have already published something on one of the main pints in dispute between the Arminians and Calvinists: and have it in view, God willing, (as I have already signified to the public), in like manner to consider all the other controverted points, and have done much towards preparation for it. But besides these, I have had on my mind and heart, (which I long ago began, not with any view to publication), a great work, which I call a *History of the Work of Redemption*, a body of divinity in an entire new method, being thrown into the form of a history, considering the affair of Christian Theology, as the whole of it in each part stands in reference to the great work of redemption by Jesus Christ, which I suppose is to be the grand design of all God's designs, and the *summum* and

133

ultimum of all the divine operations and decrees;[*] particularly considering all parts of the grand scheme in their historical order. The order of their existence, of their being brought forth to view, in the course of divine dispensations, of the wonderful series of successive acts and events; beginning from eternity, and descending from thence to the great work and successive dispensations of the infinitely wise God in time, considering the chief events coming to pass in the church of God, and revolutions in the world of mankind, affecting the state of the church and the affair of redemption, which we have an account of in history or prophecy, till at last we come to the general resurrection, last judgment and consummation of all things, when it shall be said, *It is done. I am Alpha and Omega, the Beginning and the End.* Concluding my work, with the consideration of that perfect state of things, which shall be finally settled to last for eternity. This history will be carried on with regard to all three worlds, heaven, earth and hell; considering the connected, successive events and alterations in each, so far as the Scriptures give any light; introducing all parts of divinity in that order which is most Scriptural and most natural; which is a method which appears to me the most beautiful and entertaining, wherein every divine doctrine will appear to greatest advantage in the brightest light, in the most striking manner, showing the admirable contexture and harmony of the whole.

I have also, for my own profit and entertainment, done much towards another great work, which I call *The Harmony of the Old and New Testament* in three parts. The first considering the prophecies of the Messiah, his

---

[*] "The *summum* and *ultimum* of all the divine operations and decrees," as Jonathan Edwards described it is God's overarching, inviolable plan, or in the words of an earlier New Englander, Samuel Torrey, "the Sum of all Gospel Prophesie ... in every Age and Generation ... until all the whole Mystery of God be finished, and Time shall be no longer."

redemption and kingdom, the evidences of their references to the Messiah, etc., comparing them all one with another, demonstrating their agreement and true scope and sense; also considering all the various particulars wherein these prophecies have their exact fulfillment; showing the universal, precise and admirable correspondence between predictions and events. The second part, considering the types of the Old Testament, showing the evidence of their being intended as representations of the great things of the gospel of Christ, and the agreement of the type with the antitype. The third and great part, considering the harmony of the Old and New Testament as to doctrine and precept. In the course of this work, I find there will be occasion for an explanation of a very great part of the holy Scripture; which may, in such a view be explained in a method, which to me seems the most entertaining and profitable, best tending to lead the mind to a view of the true spirit, design, life and soul of the Scriptures, as well as to their proper use and improvement.

I have also many other things in hand, in some of which I have made great progress, which I will not trouble you with an account of. Some of these things, if Divine Providence favor, I should be willing to attempt a publication of. So far as I myself am able to judge of what talents I have, for benefiting my fellow-creatures by word, I think I can write better than I can speak.

My heart is so much in these studies that I cannot find it in my heart to be willing to put myself into an incapacity to pursue them any more in the future part of my life, to such a degree as I must, if I undertake to go through the same course of employ, in the office of a president that Mr. Burr did, instructing in all the languages, and taking the whole care of the instruction of one of the classes in all parts of learning, besides his other labors. If I should see light to determine me to accept the place offered me, I should be willing to take upon me the work of a president, so far as it consists in the general inspection of the whole society, and subservient to the school, as to their order and methods of study and instruction, assisting myself in immediate instruction in the arts and sciences, (as discretion should direct and occasion serve, and the state of things require), especially the senior class; and added to all, should be willing to do the whole work of a professor of divinity, in public and private lectures, proposing questions to be answered, and some to be discussed in writing and free conversation, in meetings of graduates and others, appointed in proper seasons for these ends. It would be now out of my way to spend time in a constant teaching of the languages, unless it be the Hebrew tongue, which I should be willing to improve myself in, by instructing others.

On the whole, I am much at a loss with respect to the way of my duty in this important affair: I am in doubt, whether, if I should engage in it, I should not do what both you and I would be sorry for afterwards. Nevertheless, I think the greatness of the affair, and the regard due to so worthy and venerable a body, as that of the trustees of Nassau Hall, requires my taking the matter into serious consideration: and unless you should appear to be discouraged by the things which I have now represented, as to any further expectation from me, shall proceed to ask advice, of such as I esteem most wise, friendly and faithful: if after the mind of the commissioners in Boston is known, it appears that they consent to leave me at liberty, with respect to the business they have employed me in here.

Jonathan Edwards

~~~~~~~~~

In this suspense he determined to ask the advice of a number of gentlemen in the ministry, on whose judgment and friendship he could rely, and to act accordingly. Who upon his and his people's desire met at Stockbridge, Jan. 4, 1758. And having heard Mr. Edwards' representation of the matter, and what his people had to say by way of objection against his removal, determined it was his duty to accept of the invitation to the presidency of the college.

When they published their judgment and advice to Mr. Edwards and his people, he appeared uncommonly moved and affected with it, and fell into tears on the occasion, which was very unusual for him in the presence of others; and soon after said to the gentlemen, who had given their advice, that it was a matter of wonder to him that they could so easily, as they appeared to do, get over the objections he had made against his removal, to be the head of a college, which appeared great and weighty to him. But as he thought it his duty to be directed by their advice, he should now endeavor cheerfully to undertake it, believing he was in the way of his duty.

Accordingly, having had by the application of the trustees of the college the consent of the commissioners to resign their mission, he girded up his loins, and set off from Stockbridge for Princeton in January. He left his family at Stockbridge, not to be removed till spring. He had two daughters at Princeton, Mrs. Burr, the widow of the late President Burr, and his oldest daughter that was unmarried.

His arrival at Princeton was to the great satisfaction and joy of the college. And indeed all the greatest friends to the college, and to the interest of religion were highly satisfied and pleased with the appointment of Mr. Edwards to the presidency of that college, and had their hopes and expectations greatly raised hereby. And his correspondents, and friends, and well wishers to the college in Scotland, greatly approved of it.

The corporation met as soon as could be with convenience, after his arrival in the college, when he was by them fixed in the president's chair.

While at Princeton, before his sickness, he preached in the college hall Sabbath after Sabbath to the great acceptance of the hearers; but did nothing as president, unless it was to give out some questions in divinity to the senior class, to be answered before him; each one having opportunity to study and write what he thought proper upon them. When they came together to answer them, they found so much entertainment and profit by it, especially by the light and instruction Mr. Edwards communicated in what he said upon the questions, when they had delivered what they had to say, that they spoke of it with the greatest satisfaction and wonder.

During this time Mr. Edwards seemed to enjoy an uncommon degree of the presence of God. He told his daughters he had had great exercise, concern and fear relative to his engaging in that business; but since it now appeared, so far as he could see, that he was called of God to that place and work, he did cheerfully devote himself to it, leaving himself and the event with God to order what seemed to him good.

The small pox had now become very common in the country, and was then at Princeton, and likely to spread. And as Mr. Edwards had never had it, and inoculation was then practiced with great success in those parts, he proposed to be inoculated, if the physicians should advise to it, and the corporation would give their consent.

Accordingly, by the advice of the physician, and consent of the corporation, he was inoculated February 13. He had it favorably, and it was thought all danger was over; but a secondary fever set in, and by reason of a number of pustules in his throat, the obstruction was such that the medicines necessary to stanch the fever could not be administered. It therefore raged till it put an end to his life on the 22nd of March 1758, in the fifty-fifth year of his age.

After he was sensible that he would not survive that sickness, a little before his death, he called his daughter to him, who attended him in his sickness, and addressed her in a few words, which were immediately taken down in writing, as near as could be recollected, and are as follows:

Dear Lucy,

It seems to me to be the will of God that I must shortly leave you; therefore give my kindest love to my dear wife, and tell her that the uncommon union which has so long subsisted between us, has been of such a nature, as I trust is spiritual, and therefore will continue forever: and I hope she shall be supported under so great a trial, and submit cheerfully to the will of God. And as to my children, you are now likely to be left fatherless, which I hope will be an inducement to you all to seek a Father who will never fail you. And as to my funeral, I would have it to be like Mr. Burr's; and any additional sum of money that might be expected to be laid out that way; I would have it disposed of to charitable uses.[§]

He said but very little in his sickness; but was an admirable instance of patience and resignation to the last. Just at the close of his life as some persons who stood by, and expecting he would breath his last in a few minutes, were lamenting his death, not only as a great frown on the college, but as having a dark aspect on the interest of religion in general; to their surprise, not imagining that he heard or ever would speak another word, he said, "Trust in

---

[§] President Burr ordered, on his death bed, that his funeral should not be attended with that pomp and cost, by procuring and giving away a great number of costly mourning scarves, etc., and the consumption of a great quantity of spirituous liquors; which is an extravagance that is become too customary in those parts, especially at the funerals of the great and the rich; and that nothing should be expended but what was agreeable to the dictates of Christian decency. And that the sum which must be expended at a modish funeral, over and above the necessary cost of a decent one, should be given to the poor out of his estate.

It is to be wished and hoped, that the laudable example of these two worthy presidents, in which they bear their dying testimony against a practice so unchristian, and of such bad tendency so many ways, may have some good effect.

God, and ye need not fear." These were his last words. And what could have been more suitable to the occasion! And what need of more! In these is as much matter of instruction and support as if he had written a volume. This is the only consolation to his bereaved friends, who are sensible of the loss they and the church of Christ have sustained in his death; God is all sufficient, and still has the care of his church.

He appeared to have the uninterrupted use of his reason to the last, and died with as much calmness and composure, to all appearance, as that with which one goes to sleep.

The physician who inoculated and constantly attended him in his sickness has the following words in his letter to Mrs. Edwards on this occasion:

Never did any mortal man more fully and clearly evidence the sincerity of all his professions, by one continued, universal, calm, cheerful resignation and patient submission to the divine will, through every stage of his disease, than he. Not so much as one discontented expression, nor the least appearance of murmuring through the whole. And never did any person expire with more perfect freedom from pain: not so much as one distorted hair, but in the most proper sense of the words, he really fell asleep.

PART IV

Containing an Account of His Manuscripts, and the
Books Published by Him.

***

SECTION I

HIS MANUSCRIPTS

ℳr. Edwards has left a great many volumes in manuscript, which he wrote in a miscellaneous way on almost all subjects in divinity; which he did not with any design they should ever be published in the form in which they are; but for the satisfaction and improvement of his own mind, and that he might retain the thoughts which appeared to him worth preserving. Some idea of the progress he had made, and the materials he had collected in this way, he gives in the foregoing letter to the trustees of Nassau Hall (page 131). He has written much on the prophecies of the Messiah, justification, the divinity of Christ and the eternity of hell torments. He wrote a great deal on the Bible, in the same way, by penning his thought on particular passages of it, as they occurred to him in reading or meditation; by which he has cast much light on many parts of the Bible, which has escaped other interpreters. And by which his great and painful attention to the Bible, and making it the only rule of his faith, are manifest.

If the public were willing to be at the cost, and publishing books of divinity met with as much encouragement now, as it has sometimes, there might be a number of volumes published from his manuscripts, which would afford a great deal of new light and entertainment to

141

the church of Christ: though they would be more imperfect than if he himself had prepared them for public view.

As the method he took to have his miscellaneous writings in such order, as to be able with ease to turn to any thing he had written upon a particular subject, when he had occasion, is perhaps as good as any, if not the best that has been proposed to the public; some account of it will here be given, as what may be of advantage to young students, who have not yet gone into any method, and are disposed to improve their minds by writing.

He numbered all his miscellaneous writings. The first thing he wrote is No. 1, the second No. 2 and so on. And when he had occasion to write on any particular subject he first set down the number, and then wrote the subject in capitals or large characters that it might not escape his eye when he should have occasion to turn to it. As for instance, if he was going to write on the happiness of angels, and his last number was 148 he would begin thus—149. Angels, their happiness. And when he had written what he designed at that time on that subject, he would turn to an alphabetical table which he kept, and under the letter **A** he would write, Angels, their happiness, if this was not already in his alphabet; and then set down the number 149, close at the right hand of it. And if he had occasion to write any new thoughts on the same subject; if the number of his miscellanies were increased, so that his last number was 261, he would set the number 262, and then the subject as before. And when he had done writing for that time, he turned to his table, to the word Angels; and at the right hand of the number 149 set down 262. By this means he had no occasion to leave any chasms; but began his next subject where he left off his last.

The number of his miscellaneous writings ranged in this manner, amounts to above 1400. And yet by a table contained on a sheet or two of paper, any thing he wrote can be turned to at pleasure.

_____ *** _____

Section II

HIS PUBLICATIONS

𝔐r. Edwards was greatly esteemed and famed as an author both in Europe and America. His publications naturally raise in the reader of taste and judgment an opinion of his greatness and piety. His books met with a good reception in Scotland especially, and procured him great esteem and applause there. A gentleman of note there, for his superior genius and talents, has the following words concerning Mr. Edwards in a letter to one of his correspondents in America: "I looked on him as incomparably the greatest divine and philosopher in Britain or her colonies; and rejoiced that one so eminently qualified for teaching divinity was chosen president of New Jersey College." And in another letter the same gentleman says, "Ever since I was acquainted with Mr. Edwards' writings, I have looked upon him as the greatest divine this age has produced." And a reverend gentleman, lately from Holland says,

> That Mr. Edwards' writings, especially on the *Freedom of the Will*, was had in great esteem there: that the professors of the celebrated academy, presented their compliments to President Edwards. Several members of the classes of Amsterdam gave their thanks, by him, to pious Mr. Edwards, for his just observations on Mr. Brainerd's life;[§] which book was translated in Holland, and was highly approved of by the University of Utrecht.

[§] *Geloofwaardig Historisch Bericht, Van 't Heerlyke Werk Godts, geopenbaart in de Bekeeringe van veele honderden van Zielen, in Northampton, en op andere Plaatsen in Nieuw-Engelandt*

A brief account of what he published is therefore here subjoined. A sermon preached at Boston on 1 Corinthians 1:29, 30, 31; with a preface by one of the ministers of Boston.[x] A sermon preached at Northampton, in the year 1734, from Matthew 16:17 entitled, *A Divine and Supernatural Light Immediately Imparted to the Soul, by the Spirit of God.* The narrative[*] which has been mentioned, written Nov. 6, 1736, which was first printed in London, and recommended by Dr. (Isaac) Watts and Dr. (John) Guyse, and had two editions there. And then it had another edition in Boston, in the year 1738, recommended by four of the senior ministers[+] in Boston; to which were prefixed five discourses on the following subjects.

I. Justification by Faith Alone. II. Pressing into the Kingdom of God. III. Ruth's Resolution. IV. The Justice of God in the Damnation of Sinners. V. The Excellency of Jesus Christ; delivered at Northampton, chiefly at the time of the wonderful pouring out of the Spirit of God there.

The discourse on justification by faith alone, may be recommended as one of the best things that has been written on that subject; setting this truth in a most plain, Scriptural and convincing light; and as well worthy (of) the careful perusal of all Christians, especially candidates for the ministry. The other discourses are excellent having much divinity in them, and tending, above most that are

---

[x] *God Glorified in the Work of Redemption, by the Greatness of Man's Dependence upon Him, in the Whole of it,* This was a sermon preached on the Public Lecture in Boston, July 8, 1731.

[*] *A Faithful Narrative of the Surprizing Work of God in the Conversion of Many Hundred Souls in Northampton, and the Neighbouring Towns and Villages of New Hampshire in New England*

[+] Joseph Sewall, Thomas Prince, John Webb, William Cooper. The "Preface" is dated Nov. 4, 1738.

144

published, to awaken the conscience of the sinner, and instruct and quicken the Christian.

A sermon preached at Enfield, July 8, 1741 entitled *Sinners in the Hands of an Angry God*, preached at a time of great awakening there; and attended with remarkable impressions on many of the hearers.[*]

A sermon on *The Distinguishing Marks of a Work of the Spirit of God* preached at New Haven, September 10, 1741 from 1 John 4:1; published with great enlargements. This was reprinted in Scotland.

Some Thoughts Concerning the Present Revival of Religion in New England, And the Way in which it ought to be acknowledged and promoted, Humbly offered to the Public, in a Treatise on that Subject, in five parts; published in the year 1742. This had a second edition in Scotland.

A Treatise Concerning Religious Affections published in the year 1746. These three last have been mentioned before, with the particular occasion and design of their publication, page 87.

A treatise entitled *An Humble Attempt to Promote Explicit Agreement and Visible union of God's People in Extraordinary Prayer, for the Revival of Religion and the Advancement of Christ's Kingdom on Earth, Pursuant to Scripture Promises and Prophecies concerning the last Time*; recommended by five of the principal ministers in Boston;[§] published in 1747. In which he shows his great acquaintance with Scripture, and his attention to and good understanding of the prophetic part of it.

An Account of the Life of the Late Reverend Mr. David Brainerd, Minister of the Gospel, Missionary to the Indians,

---

[*] There were some twenty editions published by the late 1800s.

[§] Joseph Sewall, Thomas Prince, John Webb, Thomas Foxcroft, and Joshua Gee signed the "Preface" which was dated January 12, 1747/8. The publishing date was by the old style and should have been 1748.

etc. with reflections and observations thereon; published in the year 1749.*

An Humble Inquiry into the Rules of the Word of God, Concerning the Qualifications Requisite to a Complete Standing and Full Communion in the Visible Christian Church; published in the year 1749; intended as an explanation and vindication of his principles in the matter which occasioned his dismission from Northampton.

A Reply to the Rev. Mr. Solomon Williams's Book, intitled, The True State of the Question concerning the Qualifications Necessary to Lawful Communion in the Christian Sacraments; published in the year 1752.

A sermon preached at Newark, before the Synod, Sept. 28, 1752, from James 2:19, entitled, *True Grace, Distinguished from the Experience of Devils.*

A Careful and Strict Enquiry into the Modern Prevailing Notions of that Freedom of Will, which is Supposed to be Essential to Moral Agency, Virtue and Vice, Reward and Punishment, Praise and Blame; published in the year 1754.

This is justly thought, by good judges, to be one of the greatest efforts of the human mind that has appeared, at least, in this century. In which the author shows that force

---

* "Extracts from Brainerd's journal were first published by William Bradford of Philadelphia in 1746 for the Scottish Society for Propagating Christian Knowledge. Though the two parts, 'Mirabilia Dei inter Indicos' and 'Divine Grace Displayed,' have separate title pages, the signature and pagination are continuous. 'An Abridgment of Mr. David Brainerd's Journal...' was published in London in 1748. Edwards, in preparing the 'Account,' omitted such portions of the diary as had already been published. Though the Edinburgh 1765 edition of Edwards' 'Account' incorporated the portions which Edwards had originally omitted, it was not until Dwight brought out the New Haven 1822 edition that the whole was presented in chronological sequence." Thomas H. Johnson, *The Printed Writings of Jonathan Edwards: 1703-1758*, 47

and strength of mind, that judgment, penetration and accuracy of thought, that justly entitles him to the character of one of the greatest geniuses of this age. This treatise doubtless goes further towards settling the main point in controversy between Calvinists and Arminians than any thing that has been written: he having herein abundantly demonstrated the chief principles on which Arminians build their whole scheme, to be false and most absurd. Whenever, therefore, this book comes to be generally attended to, it will doubtless prove fatal to Arminian and Pelagian principles. This was reprinted in London, *Anno* 1762, and has been introduced by the Rev. T. Clap, President of Yale College, to be recited there by the students.

The great Christian Doctrine of Original Sin Defended: Evidences of It's Truth Produced, and Arguments to the Contrary Answered. Containing in Particular, a Reply to the Objections and Arguings of Dr. John Taylor, in His Book, Intitled, "The Scripture-Doctrine of Original Sin Proposed to Free and Candid Examination, etc.; published in the year 1758. This was in the press when he died.

Besides these he published several ordination sermons, and some others, preached upon particular occasions.

APPENDIX

No. I

Containing a Brief Account of Mrs. Esther Burr, and some Extracts of Letters Written by Her.

𝔐rs. Burr and her children were inoculated at the same time her father was, and were recovered when he died. But after she was perfectly recovered to all appearance she was suddenly seized with a violent disorder, which carried her out of the world in a few days; and which the physician said he could call by no name but that of *a messenger sent suddenly to call her out of the world.* She died April 7, 1758, sixteen days after her father, in the twenty-seventh year of her age. She was married to Mr. Burr June 29, 1752. By him she had two children, a son and a daughter.

Mrs. Burr exceeded most of her sex in the beauty of her person, and in a decent and easy gesture, behavior and conversation; not stiff and starch on the one hand, nor mean and indecent on the other; in her unaffected natural freedom with persons of all ranks, with whom she conversed. Her genius was much more than common. She had a lively, sprightly imagination, a quick and penetrating thought, and a good judgment. She had a peculiar smartness in her make and temper, which yet was consistent with pleasantness and good nature; and she knew how to be pleasant and facetious without trespassing on the bounds of gravity, or strict and serious religion. In short, she seemed to be formed to please, and especially to please one of Mr. Burr's taste and talents, in whom he was exceeding happy. But what crowned all her excellencies, and was her chief glory, was her religion. She was hopefully converted when she was seven or eight years old; and she made a public profession of religion where she was about fifteen years of age; and her

149

conversation and conduct to her death were exemplary, and as becomes godliness. But as her religious sentiments and exercises will best be understood by those who are strangers to her, by her own words, the following extracts are made from letters which she wrote not long before her death.

The following is an extract from a letter she wrote to her mother not long after Mr. Burr's death, dated at Princeton, October 7, 1757. After giving some account of Mr. Burr's death, and representing the sense she had of the greatness of the loss she and her children had sustained, she wrote in the following words:

> No doubt, dear madam, it will be some comfort to you to hear that God has not utterly forsaken, although he has cast down. I would speak it to the glory of God's name, that I think he has in an uncommon degree discovered himself to be an all-sufficient God, a full fountain of all good. Although all streams were cut off, yet the fountain is left full.
>
> I think I have been enabled to cast my care upon him, and have found great peace and calm in my mind, such as this world cannot give nor take.
>
> I have had uncommon freedom, and nearness to the throne of grace. God has seemed sensibly near in such a supporting and comforting manner, that I think I have never experienced the like.
>
> God has helped me to review my past and present mercies, with some heart affecting degree of thankfulness.
>
> I think God has given me such a sense of the vanity of the world, and uncertainty of all sublunary enjoyments, as I never had before. The world vanishes out of my sight! Heavenly and eternal things appear much more real and important than ever before. I feel myself to be under much greater obligations to be the Lord's than before this sore affliction.

The way of salvation by faith in Jesus Christ has appeared more clear and excellent; and I have been constrained to venture my all upon him, and have found great peace of soul, in what I hope has been actings of faith. Some parts of the Psalms have been very comforting and refreshing to my soul.

I hope God has helped me to eye his hand in this awful dispensation, and to see the infinite right he has to his own, and to dispose of them as he pleases.

Thus, dear Madam, I have given you some broken hints of the exercises and supports of my mind, since the death of him, whose memory and example will ever be precious to me as my own life.

O, dear Madam! I doubt not but I have your and my honored father's prayers daily for me; but give me leave to entreat you both to request earnestly of the Lord that I may never despise his chastenings, nor faint under this his severe stroke; which I am sensible there is great danger of, if God should only deny me the supports that he has hitherto graciously granted.

O, I am afraid I shall conduct myself so as to bring dishonor on my God, and the religion which I profess! No, rather let me die this moment than be left to bring dishonor on God's holy name. I'm overcome—I must conclude with once more begging that as my dear parents remember themselves, they would not forget their greatly afflicted daughter, (now a lonely widow), nor her fatherless children.

My duty to my ever dear and honored parents, love to my brothers and sisters. From,

Dear Madam,

Your dutiful and affectionate daughter,

ESTHER BURR

151

***

To my ever honored Father

Princeton, Nov. 2, 1757

Honored Sir,

Your most affectionate, comforting letter by my brother _____ was exceedingly refreshing to me, although I was something damped by hearing that I should not see you until spring.[§] But it is my comfort in this disappointment, as well as under all my afflictions, that God knows what is best for me, and for his own glory. Perhaps I doted too much on the company and conversation of such a near and dear affectionate father and guide. I cannot doubt but all is for the best, and I am satisfied that God should order the affair of your removal as shall be for his glory, whatever comes of me.

Since I wrote my mother's letter, God has carried me through new trials, and given me new supports. My little son has been sick with a slow fever, ever since my brother left us, and has been brought to the brink of the grave, but I hope in mercy God is bringing him up again. I was enabled to resign the child, (after a severe struggle with nature), with the greatest freedom. God showed me that the child was not my own, but his; and that he had a right to recall what he had lent, whenever he thought fit; and I had no reason to complain, or say, God was hard with me. This silenced me.

But O, how good is God! He not only kept me from complaining, but comforted me by enabling me to offer up the child by faith, I think, if ever I acted faith. I saw the fullness that was in Christ for little infants, and his willingness to accept of such as were offered to him.

[§] When Mr. Edwards wrote the letter she refers to he did not think of going to Princeton till spring; but he afterwards determined otherwise, and went in January, as is before related.

"Suffer little children to come unto me, and forbid them not," were comforting words.

God also showed me, in such a lively manner, the fullness there was in himself of all spiritual blessings, that I said, Although all streams were cut off, yet so long as my God lives, I have enough. He enabled me to say, *"Although thou slay me, yet will I trust in thee."*

In this time of trial, I was led to enter into a renewed and explicit covenant with God, in a more solemn manner than ever before; and with the greatest freedom and delight. After much self-examination and prayer, I did give up myself and children to God, with my whole heart. Never until now, had I sense of the privilege we are allowed in covenanting with God! This act of soul left my mind in a quiet and steady trust in God.

A few days after this one evening, in talking of the glorious state my dear departed husband must be in, my soul was carried out in such longing desires after this glorious state, that I was forced to retire from the family to conceal my joy. When alone, I was so transported, and my soul carried out in such eager desires after perfection, and the full enjoyment of God, and to serve him uninterruptedly, that, I think, my nature would not have borne much more. I think, dear Sir, I had, that night, a foretaste of heaven. This frame continued in some good degree the whole night. I slept but little, and when I did, my dreams were all of heavenly and divine things. Frequently since, I have felt the same in kind, though not in degree. Thus a kind and gracious God has been with me in six troubles, and in seven.

But O, Sir, what cause of deep humiliation and abasement of soul have I, on account of remaining corruption; which I see working continually, especially pride! O, how many shapes does pride cloak itself in?

Satan is also shooting his darts; but, blessed be God, those temptations of his, that used to overthrow me, as yet have not touched me. O, to be delivered from the power of

Satan, as well as sin! I cannot help hoping the time is near. God is certainly fitting me for himself; and when I think it will be soon that I shall be called hence, the thought is transporting.

No. II

Containing a Short Sketch of Mrs. Edwards' Life and Character.

℘rs. Sarah Edwards, the amiable consort of President Edwards, did not long survive him. In September she set out in a good health on a journey to Philadelphia to take care of her two orphan grandchildren, which were now in that city; and had been since the death of Mrs. Burr. As they had no relations in those parts, Mrs. Edwards proposed to take them into her own family. She arrived there, by the way of Princeton, September 21, in good health, having had a comfortable journey. But in a few days she was suddenly seized with a violent dysentery, which put an end to her life on the fifth day, October 2, 1758, in the forty-ninth year of her age. She said not much in her sickness, being exercised most of the time with violent pain. On the morning of the day she died, she apprehended her death was near, when she expressed her entire resignation to God, and desire that God might be glorified in all things; and that she might be enabled to glorify him to the last; and continued in such a temper, calm and resigned, till she died.

Her remains were carried to Princeton, which is about forty miles from Philadelphia, and deposited with Mr. Edwards'. Thus they who were in their lives remarkably lovely and pleasant, in their death were not much divided. Here lie the father and mother, the son and daughter, who were laid together in the grave, within the space of a little more than a year, though a few months before their dwelling was more than one hundred and fifty miles apart. Two presidents of the same college and their consorts, than whom it will doubtless be hard to find four persons more valuable and useful, in a few months are cut off from the earth forever; and by a remarkable providence are put, as it were, into one grave! And we, the survivors, are left under

155

the gloomy apprehension that these righteous are taken away from the evil to come.

Surely America is greatly emptied by these deaths! How much knowledge, wisdom and holiness are gone from the earth forever? And where are they who shall make good their ground?

Mrs. Edwards was born in New Haven, in Connecticut, January 9, 1709-10. Her father was the Rev. Mr. James Pierpont, who was long an eminent, godly and useful minister of the gospel at New Haven.* She was married to Mr. Edwards, July 20, 1727, in the eighteenth year of her age.

Though Mrs. Edwards' full character will not be attempted here, yet it is thought proper to mention a few things, in which she excelled, and set an example worthy the imitation of all.

She remembered her creator in the days of her youth and became truly, and remarkably religious at about five years old. Was a more than ordinary beautiful person; of a pleasant, agreeable countenance, of an amiable, courteous conversation and behavior, the law of kindness was in her tongue.

She was eminent for her piety and experimental religion. Religious conversation was much her delight and this she promoted in all companies, as far as was proper and decent for her; and her discourse showed her understanding in divine things, and the great impression they had on her mind. The friends of true religion, and they who were ready to engage in religious conversation, and delight in that which was most essential and practical in true religion, were

---

* He was the eldest son of Mr. John Pierpont of Roxbury, who came out of England. Her mother was Mrs. Mary Pierpont, eldest daughter of the Rev. Mr. Samuel Hooker, minister of the gospel at Farmington in Connecticut, and son of the Rev. Mr. Thomas Hooker, once minister of the gospel at Hartford, and famous as a divine through all the churches in England.

her peculiar friends and intimates. To whom she would open her mind freely, and tell them the exercises of her own heart, and what God had done for her soul, for their encouragement and excitement in the ways of God. Her mind appeared to them who were most conversant with her, constantly to attend to divine things, even on all occasions, and in all business of life.

The religious duties of the closet she was a great friend to, and took much delight in them. She highly prized social worship; was wont to attend the private meetings for religious worship, which were kept up at Northampton while Mr. Edwards lived there. And promoted and attended meetings of persons of her own sex only, in order for prayer and religious conversation. She was a constant attendee on public worship, and behaved with great gravity and seriousness in the house of God.

She paid proper deference to Mr. Edwards, and treated him with decency and respect at all times. As he was of a weakly, infirm constitution and was peculiar and exact in his diet, she was a tender nurse to him; cheerfully attending upon him at all times, and ministering to his comfort; and spared no pains to conform to his inclinations, and make things agreeable and comfortable to him.

She accounted it her greatest glory and that wherein she could best serve God and her generation, in being a means of promoting Mr. Edwards' comfort and usefulness in this way. And no person of discernment could be conversant in the family without observing and admiring the great harmony, and mutual love and esteem that subsisted between them.

When she herself labored under bodily disorders and pains, which was often the case, she was not wont to be full of her complaints, and put on a dejected or sour countenance, being out of humor with every body and every thing, as if she was disregarded and neglected, but she would bear up under them with patience and a kind of cheerfulness and good humor.

She was a good economist, managing her household affairs with discretion; in which she was laborious and diligent. She was very careful that nothing should be wasted and lost; and often, when she did any thing to save a small matter, or directed her children to do it in any instance, or saw them waste any thing, she would mention the words of our Saviour; which, she said, she often thought of as containing a maxim worth remembering; when, as the reason why his disciples should gather up the fragments, he said, "THAT NOTHING BE LOST." She took almost the whole care of the temporal affairs of the family, without doors and within; and in this she was peculiarly suited to Mr. Edwards' disposition, who chose to have no care of any worldly business.

She had an excellent way of governing her children: she knew how to make them regard and obey her cheerfully without loud, angry words or heavy blows. She seldom struck her children a blow; and in speaking to them, used mild, gentle and pleasant words. If any correction was needful, it was not her manner to give it in a passion. And when she had occasion to reprove and rebuke she would do it in few words, without heat and noise, with all calmness and gentleness of mind. And in her directions or reproofs, in any matters of importance, she would address herself to the reason of her children that they might not only know her inclination and will, but, at the same time, be convinced of the reasonableness of it. She need speak but once; she was cheerfully obeyed; murmuring and answering again were not known among them; and the kind and gentle treatment they had from their mother, while she strictly and punctually maintained her parental authority, seemed naturally to beget and promote a filial regard and respect, and lead them to a mild, tender treatment of each other; for quarreling and contention, as it frequently takes place among children, was not known among them. She carefully observed the first appearances of resentment and ill will towards any in her young children; and did not connive at it and promote it, as many who have the care of children do, but was careful to show her displeasure at it, and suppress it to her utmost; not by angry, wrathful words and blows, which often provoke children to wrath, and stir up and confirm their irascible passions, rather than abate and suppress them.

As she was sensible that, in many respects, the chief care of forming children by government and instruction, naturally lies on mothers, as they are most with their children in their most pliable age, when they commonly receive impressions by which they are very much formed for life; so she was very careful to do her part in this important business. And when she met with any special difficulty in this matter or foresaw any she was wont to apply to Mr. Edwards for advice and assistance; and on such occasions they would both attend to it as a matter of great importance.

But this was not all in which she expressed her care for her children. She thought that parents had great and important duty to do towards their children before they were capable of government and instruction. For them she constantly and earnestly prayed, and bore them on her heart before God, in all her secret and most solemn addresses to him; and that even before they were born. The evidence of her pregnancy, and consideration that it was with a rational, immortal creature, which came into existence in an undone, and infinitely dreadful state was sufficient to lead her to bow before God daily for his blessing on it; even redemption, and eternal life by Jesus Christ. So that through all the pain, labor and sorrow, which attended her being the mother of children, she was in travail for them that they might be born of God by having Christ formed in them.

As the law of kindness was in her tongue, so her hands were not withheld from beneficence and charity. She was always a friend and patroness of the poor and helpless, and

159

much in acts of charity, as well as recommending it to others on all proper occasions.

She was remarkable for her kindness to her friends and visitants, who resorted to Mr. Edwards. She would spare no pains to make them welcome, and provide for their convenience and comfort: and she was peculiarly kind to strangers who came to her house. She would take such kind and special notice of such, and so soon get acquainted with them, as it were, and show such regard and concern for their comfort, and so kindly offer what she thought they needed, as to discover she knew the heart of a stranger, and well understood how to do it good, and so as to oblige them to feel, in some measure, as if they were at home.

She made it her rule to speak well of all, so far as she could with truth, and justice to herself and others. She was not wont to dwell with delight on the imperfections and failings of any; and when she heard persons speaking ill of others, she would say what she thought she could with truth and justice, in their excuse or divert the obloquy by mentioning those things that were commendable in them. Thus she was tender of every one's character, even of theirs who injured and spoke evil of her; and carefully guarded against the too common vice of evil speaking and backbiting. She could bear injuries and reproach with great calmness and patience, without any disposition to render evil for evil; but, on the contrary, was ready to pity and forgive those who appeared to be her enemies.

She had long told her intimate friends, that she had after long struggles and exercises obtained, by God's grace, an habitual willingness to die herself or part with any of her most near relatives: That she was willing to bring forth children for death; and resign up him whom she esteemed so great a blessing to her and her family, her nearest partner, to the stroke of death, whenever God should see fit to take him. And when she had the greatest trial, in the death of Mr. Edwards, she found the help and comfort of such a disposition. Her conversation and conduct on this occasion was even to the admiration of her friends. It was such as discovered that she was sensible of the great loss, she and her children had sustained in his death; and at the same time showed that she was quiet and resigned, and had those invisible supports and comforts by which she could trust in God with quietness, hope and humble joy.

They lived together in the married state above thirty years. In which time they had eleven children; all which are now living, except the second daughter, who died February 14, 1748, (of whom the public have some account in the *Life of Mr. Brainerd*, page 251) and their third daughter, Mrs. Burr, before mentioned; and their youngest daughter, named Elisabeth, who died since her parents. The surviving children are three sons and five daughters.[§]

[§] This account herein published was first printed August 20, 1764. Thus this is the number of children surviving at that time. HRR

The Life and Character of Mr. Jonathan Edwards

ℱarewell 𝒮ermon·

---

^{*} What is footnoted here, by the editor, is the preface in
Volume One of *The Works of Jonathan Edwards, A.M.* that was
published in Two Volumes, it was printed by Ball, Arnold, And
Co., MDCCCXL. The preface was not in the Samuel Hopkins
volume.

A FAREWELL SERMON,
PREACHED AT THE
FIRST PRECINCT AT NORTHAMPTON
*AFTER THE PEOPLE'S PUBLIC REJECTION OF THEIR
MINISTER, AND RENOUNCING THEIR RELATION TO HIM AS
PASTOR OF THE CHURCH THERE.*
ON JUNE 32, 1750;
OCCASIONED BY DIFFERENCE OF SENTIMENTS,
CONCERNING THE REQUISITE QUALIFICATIONS OF MEMBERS
OF THE CHURCH IN COMPLETE STANDING.

Acts 20:18. Ye know, from the first day that I came into Asia, after
what manner I have been with you at all seasons

Ver. 20. And how I kept back nothing that was profitable unto you,
but have showed you, and have taught you publicly, and from house to
house.

Ver. 26, 27. Wherefore I take you to record this day, that I am pure
from the blood of all men. For I have not shunned to declare unto you all
the counsel of God.

Gal.4:15, 16. Where is then the blessedness ye speak of? For I bear
you record, that if it had been possible, ye would have plucked out your
own eyes, and haven given them to me. Am I therefore become your
enemy, because I tell you the truth?

PREFACE.

It is not unlikely, that some of the readers of the following Sermon
may be inquisitive concerning the circumstances of the difference
between me and the people of Northampton, that issued in that separation
between me and them, which occasioned the preaching of this Farewell
Sermon.—There is, by no means, room here for a full account of that
matter: but yet it seems to be proper, and even necessary, here to correct
some gross misrepresentations, which have been abundantly, and (it is to
be feared) by some affectedly and industriously made, of that difference.
Such as, that I insisted on persons being assured of their being in a state
of salvation, in order to my admitting them into the church; that I
required a particular relation of the method and order of a person's
inward experience, and of the time and manner of his conversion, as the

163

test of his fitness for Christian communion; yea, that I have undertaken to set up a pure church, and to make an exact and certain distinction between saints and hypocrites, by a pretended infallible discerning the state of men's souls; that in these things I had fallen in with those wild people, who have lately appeared in New England, called Separatists: and that I myself was become a grand separatist; that I arrogated all the power of judging of the qualifications of candidates for communion wholly to myself, and insisted on acting by my sole authority, in the admission of members into the church, &c.

In opposition to these slanderous representations, I shall at present only give my reader an account of some things which I laid before the council that separated between me and my people, in order to their having a just and full account of my principles, relating to the affair in controversy.—Long before the sitting of the council, my people had sent to the Reverend Mr. Clark of Salem Village, desiring him to write in opposition to my principles. Which gave me occasion to write to Mr. Clark, that he might have true information what my principles were. And in the time of the sitting of the council, I did, for their information, make a public declaration of my principles before them and the church, in the meeting-house, of the same import with that in my letter to Mr. Clark, and very much in the same words. And then, afterwards, sent in to the council in writing, an extract of that letter, containing the information I had given Mr. Clark, in the very words of my letter to him, that the council might read and consider it at their leisure, and have a more certain and satisfactory knowledge what my principles were. The extract which I sent in to them was in the following words:

"I am often, and I do not know but pretty generally in the country, represented as of a new and odd opinion with respect to the terms of Christian communion, and as being for introducing a peculiar way of my own.—Whereas, I do not perceive that I differ at all from the scheme of Dr. Watts, in his book entitled, *The rational Foundation of a Christian Church, and the Terms of Christian Communion*; which, he says, is the common sentiment and practice of all reformed churches. I had not seen this book of Dr. Watts when I published what I have written on the subject. But yet, I think, my sentiments, as I have expressed them, are at exactly agreeable to what he lays down, as if I had been his pupil. Nor do I at all go beyond what Dr. Doddridge plainly shows to be his sentiments, in his *Rise and Progress of Religion*, and his *Sermons on Regeneration*, and his Paraphrase and Notes on the New Testament. Nor indeed, Sir, when I consider the sentiments you have expressed in your letters to Major Pomroy and Mr. Billing, can I perceive but that they come exactly to the same thing that I maintain. You suppose, the sacraments are not converting ordinances: but that, *as seals of the covenant, they presuppose conversion especially in the adult; and that it is visible saintship, or, in other words, a credible profession of faith and repentance, a solemn consent to the gospel covenant, joined with a good conversation, and competent measure of Christian knowledge, is what gives a gospel-right to all sacred ordinances: but that it is necessary to those that come to these ordinances, and in those that profess a consent to the gospel covenant, that they be sincere in their profession* or at least should think themselves so.—The great thing which I have scrupled in the established method of this church's proceeding, and which I dare no longer go on in, is their publicly assenting to the form of words rehearsed on occasion of their admission to the communion, without pretending thereby to mean any such thing as a hearty consent to the terms of the gospel-covenant, or to mean any such faith or repentance as belong to the covenant of *grace,* and are the grand conditions of that covenant. It being, at the same time that the words are used, their known and established principle, which they openly profess and proceed, upon, that men may and ought to use these words, and mean no such thing, but something else of a nature far inferior; which I think they have no distinct determinate notion of; but something consistent with their knowing that they do not choose God as their chief good, but love the world more than him, and that they do not give themselves up entirely to God, but make reserves; and in short, knowing that they do not heartily consent to the gospel-covenant, but live still under the reigning power of the love of the world, and enmity to God and Christ. So that the words of their public profession, according to their openly established use, cease to be of the nature of any profession of gospel faith and repentance, or any proper compliance with the covenant. For it is their profession, that the words, as used, mean no such thing. The words used under these circumstances, do at least fail of being a credible profession of these things.—I can conceive of no such virtue in a certain set of words, that it is proper, merely on the making these sounds, to admit persons to Christian sacraments, without any regard to any pretended meaning of these sounds. Nor can I think, that any institution of Christ has established any such terms of admission into the Christian church.—It does not belong to the controversy between me and my people, how particular or large the profession should be that is required. I should not choose to be confined to exact limits as to that matter, but rather than contend, I should content myself with a few words, briefly expressing the cardinal virtues or acts implied in a hearty compliance with the covenant, made (as should appear by inquiry into the person's doctrinal knowledge) understanding; if there were an external conversation agreeable thereto. Yea, I should think, that such a person, solemnly making such a profession, had a right to be received as the object of a public charity, however he himself might scruple his own conversion, on account of his not remembering the time, not knowing the method, of his conversion, or finding so much remaining sin, &c. And (if his own scruples did not hinder him coming to the Lord's table) I should think the minister or church had no right to debar such a professor, though he should say he did not think himself converted. For I call that a profession of godliness, which is a profession of the great things wherein godliness consists, and not a profession of his own opinion of his good estate.

"Northampton, May 7, 1750."

The council having heard that I had made certain draughts of the covenant, or forms of a public profession of religion which I stood ready to accept of from the candidates for church communion, they, for their further information, sent for them. Accordingly I sent them four distinct draughts or forms, which I had drawn up about a twelvemonth before, as what I stood ready to accept of (any one of them) rather than contend, and break with my people.—The two shortest of these forms are here inserted for the satisfaction of the reader.—They are as follows:

"I hope I do truly find a heart to give up myself wholly to God, according to the tenor of that covenant of grace which was sealed in my baptism; and to walk in a way of obedience to all the commandments of God, which the covenant of grace requires, as long as I live." Another,

"I hope I truly find in my heart a willingness to comply with all the commandments of God, which require me to give up myself wholly to him, and to serve him with my body and my spirit. And do accordingly now promise to walk in a way of obedience to all the commandments of God, as long as I live."

Such kind of professions as these I stood ready to accept, rather than contend and break with my people Not but that I think it much more convenient, that ordinarily the public profession of religion that is made by Christians, should be much fuller and more particular And that (as I hinted in my letter to Mr. Clark) I should not choose to be tied up to any certain form of words, but to have liberty to vary the expressions of a public profession, the more exactly to suit the sentiments and experience of the professor, that it might be a more just and free expression of what each one finds in his heart.—Moreover, it must be noted, that I ever insisted on it, that it belonged to me as a pastor, before a profession was accepted, to have full liberty to instruct the candidate in the meaning of the terms of it, and in the nature of the things proposed to be professed; and to inquire into his doctrinal understanding of these things, according to my best discretion; and to caution the person, as I should think needful, against rashness in making such a profession, or doing it mainly for the credit of himself or his family, or from any secular views whatsoever, and to put him on serious self-examination, and searching his own heart and prayer to God to search and enlighten him, that he may not be hypocritical and deceived in the profession he makes; withal pointing forth to him the many ways in which professors are liable to be deceived.

Nor do I think it improper for a minister in such a case, to inquire and know of the candidate what can be remembered of the circumstances of his christian experience; as this may tend much to illustrate his

The occasion of this sermon has been mentioned in a preceding page; and is so much connected with the history of the author's life, that it was thought proper to subjoin it thereto.

2 Corinthians 1:14

As also you have acknowledged us in part, that we are your rejoicing, even as ye also are ours in the day of the Lord Jesus.

𝕿he apostle, in the preceding part of the chapter, declares what great troubles he met with in the course of his ministry. In the text, and two foregoing verses, he declares what were his comforts and supports under the troubles he met with. There are four things in particular.

---

profession, and give a minister great advantage for proper instructions: though a particular knowledge and remembrance of the time and method of the first conversion to God, is not to be made the test of a person's sincerity, nor insisted on as necessary in order to his being received into full charity. Not that I think it at all improper or unprofitable, that in some special cases, a declaration of the particular circumstances of a person's first awakening, and the manner of his convictions, illuminations, and comforts, should be publicly exhibited before the whole congregation, on occasion of his admission into the church; though this be not demanded as necessary to admission. I ever declared against insisting on a relation of experiences, in this sense, (*vis.* a relation of the particular time and steps of the operation of the Spirit, in first conversion,) as the term of communion: yet, if by a relation of experiences, be meant a declaration of experience of the great things wrought, wherein true grace and the essential acts and habits of holiness consist: in this sense, I think an account of a person's experiences necessary in order to his admission into full communion in the church. But that in whatever inquiries are made, and whatever account is given, neither minister nor church are to set up themselves as searchers of hearts, but are to accent the serious solemn profession of the well-instructed professor, of a good life, as best able to determine what he finds in his own heart. These things may serve in some measure to set right those of my readers who have been misled in their apprehensions of the state of the controversy between me and my people, by the fore mentioned misrepresentations.

1. That he had approved himself to his own conscience, 2 Corinthians 1:12. "For our rejoicing is this, the testimony of our conscience, that in simplicity and godly sincerity, not with fleshly wisdom, but by the grace of God, we have had our conversation in the world, and more abundantly to you-wards."

2. Another thing he speaks of as matter of comfort, is that as he had approved himself to his own conscience, so he had also to the consciences of his hearers, the Corinthians, to whom he now wrote, and that they should approve of him at the day of judgment.

3. The hope he had of seeing the blessed fruit of his labors and sufferings in the ministry, in their happiness and glory, in that great day of accounts.

4. That in his ministry among the Corinthians, he had approved himself to his Judge, who would approve and reward his faithfulness in that day.

These three last particulars are signified in my text, and the preceding verse, and indeed all the four are implied in the text. It is implied that the Corinthians had acknowledged him as their spiritual father, and as one that had been faithful among them, and as the means of their future joy and glory at the day of judgment. It is implied that the apostle expected at that time to have a joyful meeting with them before the Judge, and with joy to behold their glory, as the fruit of his labors, and so they would be his rejoicing. It is implied also that he then expected to be approved of the great Judge, when he and they should meet together before him, and that he would then acknowledge his fidelity, and that this had been the means of their glory, and that thus he would, as it were, give them to him as his crown of rejoicing. But this the apostle could not hope for, unless he had the testimony of his own conscience in his favor. And therefore the words do imply, in the strongest manner, that he had approved himself to his own conscience.

There is one thing implied in each of these particulars, and in every part of the text, which I shall make the subject of my present discourse, viz.

Doctrine: Ministers, and the people that have been under their care, must meet one another before Christ's tribunal at the day of judgment.

Ministers, and the people that have been under their care, must be parted in this world, how well soever they have been united. If they are not separated before, they must be parted by death, and they may be separated while life is continued. We live in a world of change, where nothing is certain or stable, and where a little time, a few revolutions of the sun, brings to pass strange things, surprising alterations, in particular persons in families, in towns and churches, in countries and nations. It often happens, that those who seem most united, in a little time are most disunited, and at the greatest distance. Thus ministers and people, between whom there has been the greatest mutual regard and strictest union, may not only differ in their judgments, and be alienated in affection, but one may rend from the other, and all relation between them be dissolved. The minister may be removed to a distant place, and they may never have any more to do one with another in this world. But if it be so, there is one meeting more that they must have, and that is in the last great day of accounts. Here I would show,

I. In what *manner* ministers, and the people which have been under their care, shall meet one another at the day of judgment.

II. For what *purposes.*

III. For what *reasons* God has so ordered it, that ministers and their people shall then meet together in such a manner, and for such purposes.

1. I would show, in some particulars, in what manner ministers and the people which have been under their care, shall meet one another at the day of judgment.

(1.) They shall not meet at the day merely as all the world must then meet together. I would observe a difference in two things.

1. As to a clear actual view, and distinct knowledge and notice, of each other.

Although the whole world will be then present, all mankind of all generations gathered in one vast assembly, with all of the angelic nature, both elect and fallen angels, yet we need not suppose that everyone will have a distinct and particular knowledge of each individual of the whole assembled multitude, which will undoubtedly consist of many millions of millions. Though it is probable that men's capacities will be much greater than in their present state, yet they will not be infinite. Though their understanding and comprehension will be vastly extended, yet men will not be deified. There will probably be a very enlarged view that particular persons will have of the various parts and members of that vast assembly, and so of the proceedings of that great day. But yet it must needs be, that according to the nature of finite minds, some persons and some things, at that day, shall fall more under the notice of particular persons than others. This (as we may well suppose) according as they shall have a nearer concern with some than others in the transactions of the day. There will be special reason why those who have had special concerns together in this world, in their state of probation, and whose mutual affairs will be then to be tried and judged, should especially be set in one another's view. Thus we may suppose, that rulers and subjects, earthly judges and those whom they have judged, neighbors who have had mutual converse, dealings, and contests, heads of families and their children and servants, shall then meet, and in a peculiar distinction be set together. And especially will it be thus with ministers and their people. It is evident by the text, that these shall be in each other's view, shall distinctly know each other, and shall have particular notice one of another at that time.

2. They shall meet together, as having special concern one with another in the great transactions of that day.

Although they shall meet the whole world at that time, yet they will not have any immediate and particular concern with all. Yea, the far greater part of those who shall then be gathered together, will be such as they have had no intercourse with in their state of probation, and so will have no mutual concerns to be judged of. But as to ministers and the people that have been under their care, they will be such as have had much immediate concern one with another, in matters of the greatest moment. Therefore they especially must meet, and be brought together before the Judge, as having special concern one with another in the design and business of that great day of accounts.—Thus their meeting, as to the manner of it, will be diverse from the meeting of mankind in general.

2. Their meeting at the day of judgment will be very diverse from their meetings one with another in this world.

Ministers and their people, while their relation continues, often meet together in this world. They are wont to meet from sabbath to sabbath, and at other times, for the public worship of God, and administration of ordinances, and the solemn services of God's house. And besides these meetings, they have also occasions to meet for the determining and managing their ecclesiastical affairs, for the exercise of church discipline, and the settling and adjusting those things which concern the purity and good order of public administrations. But their meeting at the day of judgment will be exceeding diverse, in its manner and circumstances, from any meetings and interviews they have one with another in the present state. I would observe how, in a few particulars.

1. Now they meet together in a preparatory mutable state, but then in an unchangeable state.

Now *sinners* in the congregation meet their minister in a state wherein they are capable of a saving change, capable of being turned, through God's blessing on the ministrations and labors of their pastor, from the power of Satan unto God; and being brought out of a state of guilt, condemnation, and wrath, to a state of peace and favor with God, to the enjoyment of the privileges of his children, and a title to their eternal inheritance. And saints now meet their minister with great remains of corruption, and sometimes under great spiritual difficulties and affliction: and therefore are yet the proper subjects of means for a happy alteration of their state, which they have reason to hope for in the attendance on ordinances, and of which God is pleased commonly to make his ministers the instruments. Ministers and their people now meet in order to the bringing to pass such happy changes: they are the great benefits sought in their solemn meetings.

But when they shall meet together at the day of judgment, it will be far otherwise. They will all meet in an unchangeable state. *Sinners* will be in an unchangeable state. They who then shall be under the guilt and power of sin, and have the wrath of God abiding on them, shall be beyond all remedy or possibility of change, and shall meet their ministers without any hopes of relief or remedy, or getting any good by their means. And as for the saints, they will be already perfectly delivered from all their corruption, temptation, and calamities of every kind, and set forever out of their reach; and no deliverance, no happy alteration, will remain to be accomplished in the use of means of grace, under the administrations of ministers. It will then be pronounced, "He that is unjust, let him be unjust still; and he that is filthy, let him be filthy still; and he that is righteous, let him be righteous still; and he that is holy, let him be holy still."

2. Then they shall meet together in a state of clear, certain, and infallible light.

Ministers are set as guides and teachers, and are represented in Scripture as lights set up in the churches, and in the present state meet their people, from time to time, in order to instruct and enlighten them, to correct their mistakes, and to be a voice behind them, when they turn aside to the right hand or the left, saying, "This is the way, walk ye in it;" to evince and confirm the truth by exhibiting the proper evidences of it. They to refute errors and corrupt opinions, to convince the erroneous, and establish the doubting. But when Christ shall come to judgment, every error and false opinion shall be detected. All deceit and delusion shall vanish away before the light of that day, as the darkness of the night vanishes at the appearance of the rising sun. Every doctrine of the Word of God shall then appear in full evidence, and none shall remain unconvinced. All shall know the truth with the greatest certainty, and there shall be no mistakes to rectify.

Now ministers and their people may disagree in their judgments concerning some matters of religion, and may sometimes meet to confer together concerning those things wherein they differ, and to hear the reasons that may be offered on one side and the other; and all may be ineffectual as to any conviction of the truth. They may meet and part again, no more agreed than before, and that side which was in the wrong may remain so still. Sometimes the meetings of ministers with their people, in such a case of disagreeing sentiments, are attended with unhappy debate and controversy, managed with much prejudice and want of candor; not tending to light and conviction, but rather to confirm and increase darkness, and establish opposition to the truth, and alienation of affection one from another. But when they shall meet together at the day of judgment, before the tribunal of the great Judge, the mind and will of Christ will be made known, and there shall no longer be any debate or difference of opinions. The evidence of the truth shall appear beyond all dispute, and all controversies shall be finally and forever decided.

Now ministers meet their people in order to enlighten and awaken the consciences of sinners: setting before them the great evil and danger of sin, the strictness of God's law, their own wickedness of heart and practice, the great guilt they are under, the wrath that abides upon them, and their impotence, blindness, poverty, and helpless and undone condition. But all is often in vain. They remain still, notwithstanding all their ministers can say, stupid and unawakened, and their consciences unconvinced. But it will not be so at their last meeting at the day of judgment. Sinners, when they shall meet their minister before their great Judge, will not meet him with a stupid conscience. They will then be fully convinced of the truth of those things which they formerly heard from him, concerning the greatness and terrible majesty of God, his holiness and hatred of sin, his awful justice in punishing it, the strictness of his law and the dreadfulness and truth of his threatenings, and their own unspeakable guilt and misery. And they shall never more be insensible of these things. The eyes of conscience will now be fully enlightened, and never shall be blinded again. The mouth of conscience shall now be opened, and never shall be shut any more.

Now ministers meet with their people, in public and private, in order to enlighten them concerning the state of their souls; to open and apply the rules of God's Word to them, in order to their searching their own hearts, and discerning their state. But now ministers have no infallible discernment of the state of their people; and the most skillful of them are liable to mistakes, and often are mistaken in things of this nature. Nor are the people able certainly to know the state of their minister, or one another's state: very often those pass among them for saints, and it may be eminent saints, that are grand hypocrites. And on the other hand, those are sometimes censured, or hardly received into their charity, that are indeed some of God's jewels. And nothing is more common than for men to be mistaken concerning their own state. Many that are abominable to God, and the children of his wrath, think highly of themselves, as his precious saints and dear children. Yea, there is reason to think that often some that are most bold in their confidence of their safe and happy state, and think themselves not only true saints, but the most eminent saints in the congregation, are in a peculiar manner a smoke in God's nostrils. And thus it undoubtedly often is in those congregations where the Word of God is most faithfully dispensed, notwithstanding all that ministers can say in their clearest explications, and most searching applications of the doctrines and rules of God's Word to the souls of their hearers. But in the day of judgment they shall have another sort of meeting. Then the secrets of every heart shall be made manifest, and every man's state shall be perfectly known. 1 Cor. 4:5, "Therefore judge nothing before the time, until the Lord come, who both will bring to light the hidden things of darkness, and will make manifest the counsels of the hearts: and then shall every man have praise of God." Then none shall be deceived concerning his own state, nor shall be any more in doubt about it. There shall be an eternal end to all the self-conceit and vain hopes of deluded hypocrites, and all the doubts and fears of sincere Christians. And then shall all know the state of one another's souls. The people shall know whether their minister has been sincere and faithful, and the minister shall know the state of every one of their people, and to who the word and ordinances of God have been a savor of life unto life, and to whom a savor of death unto death.

Now in this present state it often happens that when ministers and people meet together to debate and manage their ecclesiastical affairs, especially in a state of controversy, they are ready to judge and censure with regard to each other's views, designs, and the principles and ends by which each is influenced, and are greatly mistaken in their judgment and wrong one another in their censures. But at that future meeting, things will be set in a true and perfect light, and the principles and aims that everyone has acted from, shall be certainly known. There will be an end to all errors of this kind, and all unrighteous censures.

3. In this world, ministers and their people often meet together to hear of and wait upon an unseen Lord. But at the

judgment, they shall meet in his most immediate and visible presence.

Ministers, who now often meet their people to preach to them the King eternal, immortal, and invisible, to convince them that there is a God and declare to them what manner of being he is, and to convince them that he governs and will judge the world, and that there is a future state of rewards and punishments, and to preach to them a Christ in heaven, at the right hand of God, in an unseen world—shall then meet their people in the most immediate sensible presence of this great God, Savior, and Judge, appearing in the most plain, visible, and open manner, with great glory, with all his holy angels, before them and the whole world. They shall not meet them to hear about an absent Christ, an unseen Lord, and future Judge; but to appear before that Judge—being set together in the presence of that supreme Lord—in his immense glory and awful majesty, of whom they have heard so often in their meetings together on earth.

4. The meeting at the last day, of ministers and the people that have been under their care, will not be attended by anyone with a careless, heedless heart.

With such a heart are their meetings often attended in this world by many persons, having little regard to him whom they pretend unitedly to adore in the solemn duties of his public worship, taking little heed to their own thoughts or frame of their minds, not attending to the business they are engaged in, or considering the end for which they are come together. But at that great day there will not be one careless heart: no sleeping, no wandering of mind from the great concern of the meeting, no inattentiveness to the business of the day, no regardlessness of the presence they are in or of those great things which they shall hear from Christ, or that they formerly heard from him, and of him, by their ministers in their state of trial, or which they shall now hear their ministers declaring concerning them before their Judge.

176

Having observed these things, concerning the manner and circumstances of this future meeting, before the tribunal of Christ at the day of judgment, I now proceed,

II. To observe to what *purposes* they shall then meet.

1. To give an account, before the great Judge, of their behavior one to another, in the relation they bore to each other in this world.

Ministers are sent forth by Christ to their people on his business. They are his servants and messengers; and, when they have finished their service, they must return to their master to give him an account of what they have done, and of the entertainment they have had in performing their ministry. Thus we find, in Luke 14:16-21, that when the servant who was sent forth to call the guests to the great supper, had finished his appointed service, he returned to his master, and gave him an account of what he had done, and of the entertainment he had received. And when the master, being angry, sent his servant to others, he returns again and gives his master an account of his conduct and success. So we read, in Heb. 13:17, of ministers or rulers in the house of God, that "they watch for souls, as those that must give account." And we see by the forementioned Luke 14 that ministers must give an account to their master, not only of their own behavior in the discharge of their office, but also of their people's reception of them, and of the treatment they have met with among them.

Faithful ministers will then give an account with joy, concerning those who have received them well, and made a good improvement of their ministry; and these will be given them, at that day, as their crown of rejoicing. And, at the same time, they will give an account of the ill treatment of such as have not well received them and their messages from Christ. They will meet these, not as they used to do in this world, to counsel and warn them, but to bear witness against them, as their judges and assessors with Christ, to condemn them. And, on the other hand, the people will at that day rise up in judgment against wicked and unfaithful ministers, who have sought their own temporal interest more than the good of the souls of their flock.

2. At that time ministers, and the people who have been under their care, shall meet together before Christ, that he may judge between them, as to any controversies which have subsisted between them in this world.

It often comes to pass in this evil world, that great differences and controversies arise between ministers and the people under their pastoral care. Though they are under the greatest obligations to live in peace, above persons in almost any relation whatever, and although contests and dissensions between persons so related are the most unhappy and terrible in their consequences on many accounts of any sort of contentions, yet how frequent have such contentions been! Sometimes a people contest with their ministers about their doctrine, sometimes about their administrations and conduct, and sometimes about their maintenance. Sometimes such contests continue a long time, and sometimes they are decided in this world, according to the prevailing interest of one party or the other, rather than by the Word of God, and the reason of things. And sometimes such controversies never have any proper determination in this world.

But at the day of judgment there will be a full, perfect, and everlasting decision of them. The infallible Judge, the infinite fountain of light, truth, and justice, will judge between the contending parties, and will declare what is the truth, who is in the right, and what is agreeable to his mind and will. And in order hereto, the parties must stand together before him at the last day, which will be the great day of finishing and determining all controversies, rectifying all mistakes, and abolishing all unrighteous judgments, errors, and confusions, which have before subsisted in the world of mankind.

3. Ministers, and the people that have been under their care, must meet together at that time to receive an eternal sentence and retribution from the Judge, in the presence of

each other, according to their behavior in the relation they stood in one to another in the present state.

The Judge will not only declare justice, but he will do justice between ministers and their people. He will declare what is right between them, approving him that has been just and faithful, and condemning the unjust. Perfect truth and equity shall take place in the sentence which he passes, in the rewards he bestows, and the punishments which he inflicts. There shall be a glorious reward to faithful ministers, to those who have been successful. Dan. 12:3, "And they that be wise shall shine as the brightness of the firmament, and they that turn many to righteousness, as the stars for ever and ever:" and also to those who have been faithful, and yet not successful, Isa. 49:4, "Then I said, I have laboured in vain, I have spent my strength for nought; yet surely my judgment is with the Lord, and my reward with my God." And those who have well received and entertained them shall be gloriously rewarded, Matt. 10:40, 41, "He that receiveth you, receiveth me; and he that receiveth me, receiveth him that sent me. He that receiveth a prophet in the name of a prophet, shall receive a prophet's reward, and he that receiveth a righteous man, in the name of a righteous man, shall receive a righteous man's reward." Such people, and their faithful ministers, shall be each other's crown of rejoicing, 1 Thess. 2:19, 20, "For what is our hope, or joy, or crown of rejoicing? Are not even ye in the presence of our Lord Jesus Christ at his coming? For ye are our glory and joy." And in the text, "We are your rejoicing, as ye also are ours, in the day of the Lord Jesus." 2 Cor. 1:4 But they that evil entreat Christ's faithful ministers, especially in that wherein they are faithful, shall be severely punished: Matt. 10:14, 15, "And whosoever shall not receive you, nor hear your words, when ye depart out of that house or city, shake off the dust of your feet. Verily I say unto you, it shall be more tolerable for the sinners of Sodom and Gomorrah, in the day of judgment, than for that city." Deut. 33:8-11, "And of Levi he said, Let thy Thummin and thy Urim be with thy holy one. They shall teach Jacob thy judgments, and Israel thy law. Bless, Lord, his substance, and accept the work of his hands; smite through the loins of them that rise against him, and of them that hate him, that they rise not again." On the other hand, those ministers who are found to have been unfaithful, shall have a most terrible punishment. See Ez. 33:6; Mat. 23:1-33.

Thus justice shall be administered at the great day to ministers and their people: and to that end they shall meet together, that they may not only receive justice to themselves, but see justice done to the other party. For this is the end of that great day, to reveal or declare the righteous judgment of God; Rom. 2:5. Ministers shall have justice done them, and they shall see justice done to their people. And the people shall receive justice themselves from their Judge, and shall see justice done to their minister. And so all things will be adjusted and settled forever between them: everyone being sentenced and recompensed according to his works, either in receiving and wearing a crown of eternal joy and glory, or in suffering everlasting shame and pain.—I come now to the next thing proposed, viz.

III. To give some reasons why we may suppose God has so ordered it, that ministers, and the people that have been under their care, shall meet together at the day of judgment, in such a manner and for such purposes.

There are two things which I would now observe.

1. The mutual concerns of ministers and their people are of the greatest importance.

The Scripture declares that God will bring every work into judgment, with every secret thing, whether it be good or whether it be evil. It is fit that all the concerns and all the behavior of mankind, both public and private, should be brought at last before God's tribunal, and finally determined by an infallible judge. But it is especially requisite that it should be thus, as to affairs of very great importance.

Now the mutual concerns of a Christian minister and his church and congregation, are of the vastest importance: in many respects, of much greater moment than the temporal concerns of the greatest earthly monarchs, and their kingdoms or empires. It is of vast consequence how ministers discharge their office, and conduct themselves towards their people in the work of the ministry, and in affairs appertaining to it. It is also a matter of vast importance, how a people receive and entertain a faithful minister of Christ, and what improvement they make of his ministry. These things have a more immediate and direct respect to the great and last end for which man was made, and the eternal welfare of mankind, than any of the temporal concerns of men, whether private or public. And therefore it is especially fit that these affairs should be brought into judgment, and openly determined and settled, in truth and righteousness, and that to this end, ministers and their people should meet together before the omniscient and infallible Judge.

2. The mutual concerns of ministers and their people have a special relation to the main things appertaining to the day of judgment.

They have a special relation to that great and divine person who will then appear as Judge. Ministers are his messengers, sent forth by him, and in their office and administrations among their people, represent his person, stand in his stead, as those that are sent to declare his mind, to do his work, and to speak and act in his name. And therefore it is especially fit that they should return to him to give an account of their work and success. The king is judge of all his subjects, they are all accountable to him. But it is more especially requisite that the king's ministers, who are especially entrusted with the administrations of his kingdom, and who are sent forth on some special negotiation, should return to him, to give an account of themselves, and their discharge of their trust, and the reception they have met with.

Ministers are not only messengers of the person who at the last day will appear as Judge, but the errand they are sent upon, and the affairs they have committed to them as his ministers, most immediately concern his honor, and the interest of his kingdom. The work they are sent upon is to promote the designs of his administration and government, therefore their business with their people has a near relation to the day of judgment. For the great end of that day is completely to settle and establish the affairs of his kingdom, to adjust all things that pertain to it, that everything that is opposite to the interests of his kingdom may be removed, and that everything which contributes to the completeness and glory of it may be perfected and confirmed, that this great King may receive his due honor and glory.

Again, the mutual concerns of ministers and their people have a direct relation to the concerns of the day of judgment, as the business of ministers with their people is to promote the eternal salvation of the souls of men, and their escape from eternal damnation. The day of judgment is the day appointed for that end, openly to decide and settle men's eternal state, to fix some in a state of eternal salvation, and to bring their salvation to its utmost consummation, and to fix others in a state of everlasting damnation and most perfect misery. The mutual concerns of ministers and people have a most direct relation to the day of judgment, as the very design of the work of the ministry is the people's preparation for that day. Ministers are sent to warn them of the approach of that day, to forewarn them of the dreadful sentence then to be pronounced on the wicked, and declare to them the blessed sentence then to be pronounced on the righteous, and to use means with them that they may escape the wrath which is then to come on the ungodly, and obtain the reward then to be bestowed on the saints.

And as the mutual concerns of ministers and their people have so near and direct a relation to that day, it is especially fit that those concerns should be brought into that day, and there settled and issued; and that in order to this, ministers and their people should meet and appear together before the great Judge at that day.

APPLICATION

The improvement I would make of the subject is to lead the people here present, who have been under my pastoral care, to some reflections, and give them some advice suitable to our present circumstances, relating to what has been lately done in order to our being separated, but expecting to meet each other before the great tribunal at the day of judgment.

The deep and serious consideration of our future most solemn meeting, is certainly most suitable at such a time as this. There having so lately been that done, which, in all probability, will (as to the relation we have heretofore stood in) be followed with an everlasting separation.

How often have we met together in the house of God in this relation! How often have I spoke to you, instructed, counseled, warned, directed, and fed you, and administered ordinances among you, as the people which were committed to my care, and of whose precious souls I had the charge! But in all probability this never will be again.

The prophet Jeremiah (chap. 35:3), puts the people in mind how long he had labored among them in the work of the ministry: "From the thirteenth year of Josiah, the son of Amon, king of Judah, even unto this day (that is, the three and twentieth year), the word of the Lord came unto me, and I have spoken unto you, rising early and speaking." I am not about to compare myself with the prophet Jeremiah, but in this respect I can say as he did that "I have spoken the Word of God to you, unto the three and twentieth year, rising early and speaking." It was three and twenty years, the 15th day of last February, since I have labored in the work of the ministry, in the relation of a pastor to this church and congregation. And though my strength has been weakness, having always labored under great infirmity of body, besides my insufficiency for so great a charge in other respects, yet I have not spared my feeble strength, but have exerted it for the good of your souls. I can appeal to you, as the apostle does to his hearers, Gal. 4:13, "Ye know how through infirmity of the flesh, I preached the gospel unto you." I have spent the prime of my life and strength in labors for your eternal welfare. You are my witnesses that what strength I have had I have not neglected in idleness, nor laid out in prosecuting worldly schemes, and managing temporal affairs, for the advancement of my outward estate, and aggrandizing myself and family. But [I] have given myself to the work of the ministry, laboring in it night and day, rising early and applying myself to this great business to which Christ appointed me. I have found the work of the ministry among you to be a great work indeed, a work of exceeding care, labor and difficulty. Many have been the heavy burdens that I have borne in it, to which my strength has been very unequal. God called me to bear these burdens; and I bless his name that he has so supported me as to keep me from sinking under them, and that his power herein has been manifested in my weakness. So that although I have often been troubled on every side, yet I have not been distressed; perplexed, but not in despair; cast down, but not destroyed.—But now I have reason to think my work is finished which I had to do as your minister: you have publicly rejected me, and my opportunities cease.

How highly therefore does it now become us to consider of that time when we must meet one another before the chief Shepherd! When I must give an account of my stewardship, of the service I have done for, and the reception and treatment I have had among the people to whom he sent me. And you must give an account of your own conduct towards me, and the improvement you have made of these three and twenty years of my ministry. For then both you and I must appear together, and we both must give an account, in order to an infallible, righteous and eternal sentence to be passed upon us, by him who will judge us with respect to all that we have said or done in our meeting here, and all our conduct one towards another in the house of God and elsewhere. [He] will try our hearts, and manifest our thoughts, and the principles and frames of our minds. He will judge us with respect to all the controversies which have subsisted between us, with the strictest impartiality, and will examine our treatment of each other in those controversies. There is nothing covered that shall not be revealed, nor hid which shall not be known. All will be examined in the searching, penetrating light of God's omniscience and glory, and by him whose eyes are as a flame of fire. Truth and right shall be made plainly to appear, being stripped of every veil. And all error, falsehood, unrighteousness, and injury shall be laid open, stripped of every disguise. Every specious pretense, every cavil, and all false reasoning shall vanish in a moment, as not being able to bear the light of that day. And then our hearts will be turned inside out, and the secrets of them will be made more plainly to appear than our outward actions do now. Then it shall appear what the ends are which we have aimed at, what have been the governing principles which we have acted from, and what have been the dispositions we have exercised in our ecclesiastical disputes and contests. Then it will appear whether I acted uprightly, and from a truly conscientious, careful regard to my duty to my great Lord and Master, in some former ecclesiastical controversies, which have been attended with exceeding unhappy circumstances and consequences. It will appear whether there was any just cause for the resentment which was manifested on those occasions. And then our late grand controversy, concerning the qualifications necessary for admission to the privileges of members, in complete standing, in the visible church of Christ, will be examined and judged in all its parts and circumstances, and the whole set forth in a clear, certain, and perfect light. Then it will appear whether the doctrine which I have preached and published concerning this matter be Christ's own doctrine, whether he will not own it as one of the precious truths which have proceeded from his own mouth, and vindicate and honor as such before the whole universe. Then it will appear what is meant by "the man that comes without the wedding garment;" for that is the day spoken of, Mat. 22:13, wherein such a one shall be "bound hand and foot, and cast into outer darkness, where shall be weeping and gnashing of teeth." And then it will appear whether, in declaring this doctrine, and acting agreeable to it, and in my general conduct in the affair, I have been influenced from any regard to my own temporal interest, or honor, or desire to appear wiser than others, or have acted from any sinister, secular views whatsoever, and whether what I have done has not been from a careful, strict, and tender regard to the will of my Lord and Master, and because I dare not offend him, being satisfied what his will was, after a long, diligent, impartial, and prayerful inquiry. Then it will be seen whether I had this constantly in view and prospect, to engage me to great solicitude not rashly to determine the question, that such a determination would not be for my temporal interest, but every way against it, bringing a long series of extreme difficulties, and plunging me into an abyss of trouble and sorrow. And then it will appear whether my people have done their duty to their pastor with respect to this matter; whether they have shown a right temper and spirit on this occasion; whether they have done me justice in hearing, attending to and considering what I had to say in evidence of what I believed and taught as part of the counsel of God; whether I have been treated with that impartiality, candor, and regard which the just Judge esteemed due; and whether, in the many steps which have been taken, and the many things that have been said and done in the course of this controversy, righteousness, and charity, and Christian decorum have been maintained; or, if otherwise, to how great a degree these things have been violated. Then every step of the conduct of each of us in this affair, from first to last, and the spirit we have exercised in all, shall be examined and manifested, and our own consciences shall speak plain and loud, and each of us shall be convinced, and the world shall know; and never shall there be any more mistake, misrepresentation, or misapprehension of the affair to eternity.

This controversy is now probably brought to an issue between you and me as to this world. It has issued in the event of the week before last, but it must have another decision at that great day, which certainly will come, when you and I shall meet together before the great judgment seat. Therefore I leave it to that time, and shall say no more about it at present.—But I would now proceed to address myself particularly to several sorts of persons.

I. To those who are *professors* of godliness amongst us.

I would now call you to a serious consideration of that great day wherein you must meet him who has heretofore been your pastor, before the Judge whose eyes are as a flame of fire.—I have endeavored, according to my best ability, to search the Word of God, with regard to the distinguishing notes of true piety, those by which persons might best discover their state, and most surely and clearly judge of themselves. And these rules and marks I have from time to time applied to you, in the preaching of the Word to the utmost of my skill, and in the most plain and searching manner that I have been able, in order to the detecting the deceived hypocrite, and establishing the hopes and comforts of the sincere. And yet it is to be feared, that after all that I have done, I now leave some of you in a deceived, deluded state. For it is not to be supposed that among several hundred professors, none are deceived.

Henceforward I am like to have no more opportunity to take the care and charge of your souls, to examine and search them. But still I entreat you to remember and consider the rules which I have often laid down to you during my ministry, with a solemn regard to the future day when you and I must meet together before our Judge, when the uses of examination you have heard from me must be rehearsed again before you, and those rules of trial must be tried, and it will appear whether they have been good or not. It will also appear whether you have impartially heard them, and tried yourselves by them. The Judge himself, who is infallible, will try both you and me. And after this none will be deceived concerning the state of their souls.

I have often put you in mind, that whatever your pretenses to experiences, discoveries, comforts, and joys have been, at that day everyone will be judged according to his works, and then you will find it so. May you have a minister of greater knowledge of the Word of God, and better acquaintance with soul cases, and of greater skill in applying himself to souls, whose discourses may be more searching and convincing, that such of you as have held fast deceit under my preaching, may have your eyes opened by his: that you may be undeceived before that great day.

What means and helps for instruction and self-examination you may hereafter have is uncertain. But one thing is certain: that the time is short, your opportunity for rectifying mistakes in so important a concern will soon come to an end. We live in a world of great changes. There is now a great change come to pass. You have withdrawn yourselves from my ministry, under which you have continued for so many years. But the time is coming, and will soon come, when you will pass out of time into eternity, and so will pass from under all means of grace whatsoever.

The greater part of you who are professors of godliness have (to use the phrase of the apostle) "acknowledged me, in part:" you have heretofore acknowledged me to be your spiritual father, the instrument of the greatest good to you that can be obtained by any of the children of men. Consider of that day when you and I shall meet before our Judge, when it shall be examined whether you have had from me the treatment which is due to spiritual children, and whether

188

you have treated me as you ought to have treated a spiritual father.—As the relation of a natural parent brings great obligations on children in the sight of God, so much more, in many respects, does the relation of a spiritual father bring great obligations on such of whose conversation and eternal salvation they suppose God has made them the instruments, 1 Cor. 4:15, "For though you have ten thousand instructors in Christ, yet have ye not many fathers: for in Christ Jesus, I have begotten you through the gospel."

II. Now I am taking my leave of this people I would apply myself to such among them as I leave in a Christless, graceless condition, and would call on such seriously to consider of that solemn day when they and I must meet before the Judge of the world.

My parting with you is, in some respects, in a peculiar manner a melancholy parting, inasmuch as I leave you in most melancholy circumstances, because I leave you in the gall of bitterness and bond of iniquity, having the wrath of God abiding on you, and remaining under condemnation to everlasting misery and destruction. Seeing I must leave you, it would have been a comfortable and happy circumstance of our parting, if I had left you in Christ, safe and blessed in that sure refuge and glorious rest of the saints. But it is otherwise. I leave you far off, aliens and strangers, wretched subjects and captives of sin and Satan, and prisoners of vindictive justice: without Christ, and without God in the world.

Your consciences bear me witness that while I had opportunity, I have not ceased to warn you, and set before you your danger. I have studied to represent the misery and necessity of your circumstances in the clearest manner possible. I have tried all ways that I could think of tending to awaken your consciences, and make you sensible of the necessity of your improving your time, and being speedy in flying from the wrath to come, and thorough in the use of means for your escape and safety. I have diligently endeavored to find out and use the most powerful motives

189

to persuade you to take care for your own welfare and salvation. I have not only endeavored to awaken you, that you might be moved with fear, but I have used my utmost endeavors to win you: I have sought out acceptable words, that if possible I might prevail upon you to forsake sin, and turn to God, and accept of Christ as your Savior and Lord. I have spent my strength very much in these things. But yet, with regard to you whom I am addressing, I have not been successful, but have this day reason to complain in those words, Jer. 6:29, "The bellows are burnt, the lead is consumed of the fire, the founder melteth in vain, for the wicked are not plucked away." It is to be feared that all my labors, as to many of you, have served no other purpose but to harden you, and that the word which I have preached, instead of being a savor of life unto life, has been a savor of death unto death. Though I shall not have any account to give for the future of such as have openly and resolutely renounced my ministry, as of a trust committed to me, yet remember you must give account for yourselves, of your care of your own souls, and your improvement of all means past and future, through your whole lives. God only knows what will become of your poor perishing souls, what means you may hereafter enjoy, or what disadvantages and temptations you may be under. May God in his mercy grant that however all past means have been unsuccessful, you may have future means which may have a new effect, and that the Word of God, as it shall be hereafter dispensed to you, may prove as the fire and the hammer that breaketh the rock in pieces. However, let me now at parting exhort and beseech you not wholly to forget the warnings you have had while under my ministry. When you and I shall meet at the day of judgment, then you will remember them. The sight of me, your former minister, on that occasion, will soon revive them in your memory; and that in a very affecting manner. O do not let that be the first time that they are so revived.

You and I are now parting one from another as to this world. Let us labour that we may not be parted after our meeting at the last day. If I have been your faithful pastor (which will that day appear whether I have or no), then I shall be acquitted, and shall ascend with Christ. O do your part that in such a case, you may not be forced eternally to part from me, and all that have been faithful in Christ Jesus. *This* is a sorrowful parting, but *that* would be a more sorrowful.—This you may perhaps bear without being much affected with it, if you are not glad of it, but such a parting in that day will most deeply, sensibly, and dreadfully affect you.

III. I would address myself to those who are under some *awakenings*.

Blessed be God that there are some such, and that (although I have reason to fear I leave multitudes in this large congregation in a Christless state) yet I do not leave them all in total stupidity and carelessness about their souls. Some of you that I have reason to hope are under some awakenings, have acquainted me with your circumstances, which has a tendency to cause me, now I am leaving you, to take my leave with peculiar concern for you. What will be the issue of your present exercise of mind, I know not, but it will be known at that day, when you and I shall meet before the judgment seat of Christ. Therefore now be much in consideration of that day.

Now I am parting with this flock, I would once more press upon you the counsels I have heretofore given, to take heed of slighting so great a concern, to be thorough and in good earnest in the affair, and to beware of backsliding, to hold on and hold out to the end. And cry mightily to God, that these great changes which pass over this church and congregation do not prove your overthrow. There is great temptation in them, and the devil will undoubtedly seek to make his advantage of them, if possible to cause your present convictions and endeavors to be abortive. You had need to double your diligence, and watch and pray, lest you be overcome by temptation.

Whoever may hereafter stand related to you as your spiritual guide, my desire and prayer is that the great Shepherd of the sheep would have a special respect to you, and be your guide (for there is none teacheth like him), and that he who is the infinite fountain of light, would "open your eyes, and turn you from darkness unto light, and from the power of Satan unto God; that you may receive forgiveness of sins, and inheritance among them that are sanctified, through faith that is in Christ;" that so in that great day, when I shall meet you again before your Judge and mine, we may meet in joyful and glorious circumstances, never to be separated any more.

IV. I would apply myself to the *young* people of the congregation.

Since I have been settled in the work of the ministry in this place, I have ever had a peculiar concern for the souls of the young people, and a desire that religion might flourish among them; and have especially exerted myself in order to it. Because I knew the special opportunity they had beyond others, and that ordinarily those for whom God intended mercy, were brought to fear and love him in their youth. And it has ever appeared to me a peculiarly amiable thing, to see young people walking in the ways of virtue and Christian piety, having their hearts purified and sweetened with a principle of divine love. How exceeding beautiful, and conducive to the adorning and happiness of the town, if the young people could be persuaded, when they meet together, to converse as Christians and as the children of God, avoiding impurity, levity and extravagance, keeping strictly to rules of virtue and conversing together of the things of God, and Christ, and heaven! This is what I have longed for, and it has been exceeding grievous to me when I have heard of vice, vanity and disorder among our youth. And so far as I know my own heart, it was from hence that I formerly led this church to some measures, for the suppressing vice among our young people, which gave so great offense, and by which I became so obnoxious. I have sought the good, and not the hurt of our young people. I have desired their truest honor and happiness, and not their reproach: knowing that true virtue and religion tended not only to the glory and felicity of young people in another world, but their greatest peace and prosperity, and highest dignity and honor in this world, and above all things to sweeten, and render pleasant and delightful, even the days of youth.

But whether I have loved you, and sought your good more or less, now committing your souls to him who once committed the pastoral care of them to me—nothing remains, but only (as I am now taking my leave of you) earnestly to beseech you, from love to yourselves, if you have none to me, not to despise and forget the warnings and counsels I have so often given you. Remember the day when you and I must meet again before the great Judge of quick and dead, when it will appear whether the things I have taught you were true, whether the counsels I have given you were good, and whether I truly sought your welfare, and whether you have well improved my endeavors.

I have, from time to time, earnestly warned you against *frolicking* (as it is called), and some other liberties commonly taken by young people in the land. And whatever some may say in justification of such liberties and customs, and may laugh at warnings against them, I now leave you my parting testimony against such things, not doubting but God will approve and confirm it in that day when we shall meet before him.

V. I would apply myself to the *children* of the congregation, the lambs of this flock, who have been so long under my care.

I have just now said that I have had a peculiar concern for the young people, and in so saying I did not intend to exclude you. You are in youth, and in the most early youth. Therefore I have been sensible that if those that were young had a precious opportunity for their souls' good, you who are very young had, in many respects, a peculiarly precious opportunity. And accordingly I have not neglected you. I have endeavored to do the part of a faithful shepherd, in feeding the lambs as well as the sheep. Christ did once commit the care of your souls to me as your minister; and you know, dear children, how I have instructed you, and warned you from time to time. You know how I have often called you together for that end, and some of you, sometimes, have seemed to be affected with what I have said to you. But I am afraid it has had no saving effect as to many of you, but that you remain still in an unconverted condition, without any real saving work wrought in your souls, convincing you thoroughly of your sin and misery, causing you to see the great evil of sin, and to mourn for it, and hate it above all things, and giving you a sense of the excellency of the Lord Jesus Christ, bringing you with all your hearts to cleave to him as your Savior, weaning your hearts from the world, and causing you to love God above all, and to delight in holiness more than in all the pleasant things of this earth. And I must now leave you in a miserable condition, having no interest in Christ, and so under the awful displeasure and anger of God, and in danger of going down to the pit of eternal misery.—Now I must bid you farewell. I must leave you in the hands of God. I can do no more for you than to pray for you. Only I desire you not to forget, but often think of the counsels and warnings I have given you, and the endeavors I have used, that your souls might be saved from everlasting destruction.

Dear children, I leave you in an evil world, that is full of snares and temptations. God only knows what will become of you. This the Scripture has told us that there are but few saved, and we have abundant confirmation of it from what we see. This we see, that children die as well as others. Multitudes die before they grow up, and of those that grow up, comparatively few ever give good evidence of saving conversion to God. I pray God to pity you, and take care of you, and provide for you the best means for the good of your souls, and that God himself would undertake for you to be your heavenly Father, and the mighty Redeemer of your immortal souls. Do not neglect to pray for yourselves. Take heed you be not of the number of those who cast off fear, and restrain prayer before God. Constantly pray to God in secret, and often remember that great day when you must appear before the judgment seat of Christ, and meet your minister there, who has so often counseled and warned you.

I conclude with a few words of advice to all in general, in some particulars, which are of great importance in order to the future welfare and prosperity of this church and congregation.

1. One thing that greatly concerns you, as you would be a happy people, is the maintaining of *family order.*

We have had great disputes how the church ought to be regulated; and indeed the subject of these disputes was of great importance: but the due regulation of your families is of no less, and, in some respects, of much greater importance. Every Christian family ought to be as it were a little church, consecrated to Christ, and wholly influenced and governed by his rules. And family education and order are some of the chief of the means of grace. If these fail, all other means are likely to prove ineffectual. If these are duly maintained, all the means of grace will be likely to prosper and be successful.

Let me now therefore, once more, before I finally cease to speak to this congregation, repeat, and earnestly press the counsel which I have often urged on heads of families, while I was their pastor, to great painfulness in teaching, warning, and directing their children; bringing them up in the nurture and admonition of the Lord; beginning early, where there is yet opportunity, and maintaining a constant diligence in labours of this kind. Remember that, as you would not have all your instructions and counsels ineffectual, there must be government as well as instructions, which must be maintained with an even hand,

and steady resolution, as a guard to the religion and morals of the family, and the support of its good order. Take heed that it be not with any of you as it was with Eli of old, who reproved his children, but restrained them not; and that, by this means, you do not bring the like curse on your families as he did on his.

And let children obey their parents, and yield to their instructions, and submit to their orders, as they would inherit a blessing and not a curse. For we have reason to think, from many things in the word of God, that nothing has a greater tendency to bring a curse on persons in this world, and on all their temporal concerns, than an undutiful, unsubmissive, disorderly behaviour in children towards their parents.

2. As you would seek the future prosperity of this society, it is of vast importance that you should avoid contention.

A contentious people will be a miserable people. The contentions which have been among you. since I first became your pastor, have been one of the greatest burdens I have laboured under in the course of my ministry—not only the contentions you have had with me, but those which you have had one with another, about your lands, and other concerns—because I knew that contention, heat of spirit, evil speaking, and things of the like nature, were directly contrary to the spirit of Christianity, and did, in a peculiar manner, tend to drive away God's Spirit from a people, and to render all means of grace ineffectual, as well as to destroy a people's outward comfort and welfare.

Let me therefore earnestly exhort you, as you would seek your own future good, hereafter to watch against a contentious spirit. "If you would see good days, seek peace, and ensue it," 1 Pet. 3:10, 11. Let the late contention about the terms of Christian communion, as it has been the greatest, be the last. I would, now I am preaching my farewell sermon, say to you, as the apostle to the Corinthians, 2 Cor. 13:11, "Finally, brethren, farewell. Be perfect, be of one mind, live in peace; and the God of love and peace shall be with you."

And here I would particularly advise those that have adhered to me in the late controversy, to watch over their spirits, and avoid all bitterness towards others. Your temptations are, in some respects, the greatest; because what has been lately done is grievous to you. But however wrong you may think others have done, maintain, with great diligence and watchfulness, a Christian meekness and sedateness of spirit; and labour, in this respect, to excel others who are of the contrary part. And this will be the best victory: for "he that rules his spirit, is better than he that takes a city." Therefore let nothing be done through strife or vain-glory. Indulge no revengeful spirit in any wise; but watch and pray against it: and, by all means in your power, seek the prosperity of this town. And never think you behave yourselves as becomes Christians, but when you sincerely, sensibly, and fervently love all men, of whatever party or opinion, and whether friendly or unkind, just or injurious, to you or your friends, or to the cause and kingdom of Christ.

3. Another thing that vastly concerns the future prosperity of the town, is, that you should watch against the encroachments of error; and particularly Arminianism, and doctrines of like tendency.

You were, many of you, as I well remember, much alarmed with the apprehension of the danger of the prevailing of these corrupt principles, near sixteen years ago. But the danger then was small in comparison of what appears now. These doctrines at this day are much more prevalent than they were then. The progress they have made in the land, within this seven years, seems to have been vastly greater than at any time in the like space before. And they are still prevailing and creeping into almost all parts of the land, threatening the utter ruin of the credit of those doctrines which are the peculiar glory of the gospel, and the interests of vital piety. And I have of late perceived some

197

things among yourselves, that show that you are far from being out of danger, but on the contrary remarkably exposed. The elder people may perhaps think themselves sufficiently fortified against infection. But it is fit that all should beware of self-confidence and carnal security, and should remember those needful warnings of sacred writ, "Be not high minded, but fear; and let him that stands, take heed lest he fall." But let the case of the elder people be as it will, the rising generation are doubtless greatly exposed. These principles are exceeding taking with corrupt nature, and what young people, at least such as have not their hearts established with grace, are easily led away with.

And if these principles should greatly prevail in this town, as they very lately have done in another large town I could name, formerly greatly noted for religion, for a long time, it will threaten the spiritual and eternal ruin of this people, in the present and future generations. Therefore you have need of the greatest and most diligent care and watchfulness with respect to this matter.

4. Another thing which I would advise to, that you may hereafter be a prosperous people, is, that you would give yourselves much to prayer.

God is the fountain of all blessing and prosperity, and he will be sought to for his blessing. I would therefore advise you not only to be constant in secret and family prayer, and in the public worship of God in his house, but also often to assemble yourselves in private praying societies. I would advise all such as are grieved for the afflictions of Joseph, and sensibly affected with the calamities of this town, of whatever opinion they be with relation to the subject of our late controversy, often to meet together for prayer, and cry to God for his mercy to themselves, and mercy to this town, and more to Zion and the people of God in general through the world.

5. The last article of advice I would give (which doubtless does greatly concern your prosperity) is, that you

would take great care with regard to the settlement of a minister; and particularly in these two respects.

(1.) That he be a man of thoroughly sound principles, in the scheme of doctrine which he maintains.

Of this you will stand in the greatest need, especially at such a day of corruption as this is. And in order to obtain such a one, you had need to exercise extraordinary care and prudence.—I know the danger.—I know the manner of many young gentlemen of corrupt principles, their ways of concealing themselves, the fair specious disguises they are wont to put on, by which they deceive others, to maintain their own credit, and get themselves into others' confidence, and establish their own interest, until they see a convenient opportunity to begin more openly to broach and propagate their corrupt tenets.

(2.) Labor to obtain a man who has an established character, as a person of serious religion and fervent piety.

It is of vast importance that those who are settled in this work should be men of true piety, at all times, and in all places; but more especially at some times, and in some towns and churches. And this present time, which is a time wherein religion is in danger, by so many corruptions in doctrine and practice, is in a peculiar manner a day wherein such ministers are necessary. Nothing else but sincere piety of heart is at all to be depended on, as a security to a young man, just coming into the world, from the prevailing infection, or thoroughly to engage him in proper and successful endeavours to withstand and oppose the torrent of error and prejudice, against the high mysterious evangelical doctrines of the religion of Jesus Christ, and their genuine effects in true experimental religion. And this is a place that does peculiarly need such a minister, for reasons obvious to all.

If you should happen to settle a minister who knows nothing truly of Christ, and the way of salvation by him, nothing experimentally of the nature of vital religion, alas, how will you be exposed as sheep without a shepherd! Here is need of one who shall be eminently fit to stand in the gap, and make up the hedge, and who shall be as the chariots of Israel, and the horsemen thereof. You need one that shall stand as champion in the cause of truth and the power of godliness.

Having briefly mentioned these important articles of advice, nothing remains, but that I now take my leave of you, and bid you all *farewell*; wishing and praying for your best prosperity. 1 would now commend your immortal souls to him, who formerly committed them to me, expecting the day when I must meet you again before him, who is the Judge of quick and dead. I desire that I may never forget this people, who have been so long my special charge, and that I may never cease fervently to pray for your prosperity. May God bless you with a faithful pastor, one that is well acquainted with his mind and will, thoroughly warning sinners, wisely and skillfully searching professors, and conducting you in the way to eternal blessedness. May you have truly a burning and shining light set up in this candlestick; and may you, not only for a season, but during his whole life, that a long life, be willing to rejoice in his light.

And let me be remembered in the prayers of all God's people that are of a calm spirit, and are peaceable and faithful in Israel, of whatever opinion they may be with respect to terms of church communion. And let us all remember, and never forget our future solemn meeting on that great day of the Lord; the day of infallible decision, and of the everlasting and unalterable sentence. Amen.

Sinners in the Hands of an Angry God*

Deut 32:35

Their foot shall slide in due time.

In this verse is threatened the vengeance of God on the wicked unbelieving Israelites, who were God's visible people, and who lived under the means of grace; but who, notwithstanding all God's wonderful works towards them, remained (as Deut 32:28) void of counsel, having no understanding in them. Under all the cultivations of heaven, they brought forth bitter and poisonous fruit; as in the two verses next preceding the text.—The expression I have chosen for my text, *their foot shall slide in due time,* seems to imply the following things, relating to the punishment and destruction to which these wicked Israelites were exposed.

1. That they were always exposed to *destruction*; as one that stands or walks in slippery places is always exposed to fall. This is implied in the manner of their destruction coming upon them, being represented by their foot sliding. The same is expressed, Ps 73:18, "Surely thou didst set them in slippery places; thou castedst them down into destruction."

---

* Preached at Enfield, July 8, 1741, at a time of great awakenings, and attended with remarkable impressions on many of the hearers. This sermon was not in the Hopkins edition, but has been added to the Sprinkle edition for the reader.

2. It implies that they were always exposed to sudden unexpected destruction. As he that walks in slippery places is every moment liable to fall, he cannot foresee one moment whether he shall stand or fall the next; and when he does fall, he falls at once without warning: Which is also expressed in Ps 73:18-19, "Surely thou didst set them in slippery places; thou castedst them down into destruction: How are they brought into desolation as in a moment?"

3. Another thing implied is, that they are liable to fall *of themselves*, without being thrown down by the hand of another; as he that stands or walks on slippery ground needs nothing but his own weight to throw him down.

4. That the reason why they are not fallen already and do not fall now is only that God's appointed time is not come. For it is said, that when that due time, or appointed time comes, *their foot shall slide*. Then they shall be left to fall, as they are inclined by their own weight. God will not hold them up in these slippery places any longer, but will let them go; and then, at that very instant, they shall fall into destruction; as he that stands on such slippery declining ground, on the edge of a pit, he cannot stand alone, when he is let go he immediately falls and is lost.

The observation from the words that I would now insist upon is this.—"There is nothing that keeps wicked men at any one moment out of hell, but the mere pleasure of God."—By the *mere* pleasure of God, I mean his *sovereign* pleasure, his arbitrary will, restrained by no obligation, hindered by no manner of difficulty, any more than if nothing else but God's mere will had in the least degree, or in any respect whatsoever, any hand in the preservation of wicked men one moment.—The truth of this observation may appear by the following considerations.

1. There is no want of *power* in God to cast wicked men into hell at any moment. Men's hands cannot be strong when God rises up. The strongest have no power to resist him, nor can any deliver out of his hands.—He is not only able to cast wicked men into hell, but he can most easily do

it. Sometimes an earthly prince meets with a great deal of difficulty to subdue a rebel, who has found means to fortify himself, and has made himself strong by the numbers of his followers. But it is not so with God. There is no fortress that is any defense from the power of God. Though hand join in hand, and vast multitudes of God's enemies combine and associate themselves, they are easily broken in pieces. They are as great heaps of light chaff before the whirlwind; or large quantities of dry stubble before devouring flames. We find it easy to tread on and crush a worm that we see crawling on the earth; so it is easy for us to cut or singe a slender thread that any thing hangs by: thus easy is it for God, when he pleases, to cast his enemies down to hell. What are we, that we should think to stand before him, at whose rebuke the earth trembles, and before whom the rocks are thrown down?

2. They *deserve* to be cast into hell; so that divine justice never stands in the way, it makes no objection against God's using his power at any moment to destroy them. Yea, on the contrary, justice calls aloud for an infinite punishment of their sins. Divine justice says of the tree that brings forth such grapes of Sodom, "Cut it down, why cumbereth it the ground?" Luke 13:7. The sword of divine justice is every moment brandished over their heads, and it is nothing but the hand of arbitrary mercy, and God's mere will, that holds it back.

3. They are already under a sentence of *condemnation* to hell. They do not only justly deserve to be cast down thither, but the sentence of the law of God, that eternal and immutable rule of righteousness that God has fixed between him and mankind, is gone out against them, and stands against them; so that they are bound over already to hell. John 3:18, "He that believeth not is condemned already." So that every unconverted man properly belongs to hell; that is his place; from thence he is, John 8:23, "Ye are from beneath," and thither he is bound; it is the place that justice,

and God's word, and the sentence of his unchangeable law, assign to him.

4. They are now the objects of that very same *anger* and wrath of God that is expressed in the torments of hell. And the reason why they do not go down to hell at each moment, is not because God, in whose power they are, is not then very angry with them; as he is with many miserable creatures now tormented in hell, who there feel and bear the fierceness of his wrath. Yea, God is a great deal more angry with great numbers that are now on earth; yea, doubtless, with many that are now in this congregation, who it may be are at ease, than he is with many of those who are now in the flames of hell.—So that it is not because God is unmindful of their wickedness, and does not resent it, that he does not let loose his hand and cut them off. God is not altogether such an one as themselves, though they may imagine him to be so. The wrath of God burns against them, their damnation does not slumber; the pit is prepared, the fire is made ready, the furnace is now hot, ready to receive them; the flames do now rage and glow. The glittering sword is whet, and held over them, and the pit hath opened its mouth under them.

5. The *devil* stands ready to fall upon them, and seize them as his own, at what moment God shall permit him. They belong to him; he has their souls in his possession, and under his dominion. The Scripture represents them as his goods, Luke 11:12. The devils watch them; they are ever by them at their right hand; they stand waiting for them, like greedy hungry lions that see their prey, and expect to have it, but are for the present kept back. If God should withdraw his hand, by which they are restrained, they would in one moment fly upon their poor souls. The old serpent is gaping for them; hell opens its mouth wide to receive them; and if God should permit it, they would be hastily swallowed up and lost.

6. There are in the souls of wicked men those hellish *principles* reigning, that would presently kindle and flame

out into hellfire, if it were not for God's restraints. There is laid in the very nature of carnal men, a foundation for the torments of hell. There are those corrupt principles, in reigning power in them, and in full possession of them, that are seeds of hellfire. These principles are active and powerful, exceeding violent in their nature, and if it were not for the restraining hand of God upon them, they would soon break out, they would flame out after the same manner as the same corruptions, the same enmity does in the hearts of damned souls, and would beget the same torments as they do in them. The souls of the wicked are in Scripture compared to the troubled sea, Isa. 57:20. For the present, God restrains their wickedness by his mighty power, as he does the raging waves of the troubled sea, saying, "Hitherto shalt thou come, but no further," but if God should withdraw that restraining power, it would soon carry all before it. Sin is the ruin and misery of the soul; it is destructive in its nature; and if God should leave it without restraint, there would need nothing else to make the soul perfectly miserable. The corruption of the heart of man is immoderate and boundless in its fury; and while wicked men live here, it is like fire pent up by God's restraints, whereas if it were let loose, it would set on fire the course of nature; and as the heart is now a sink of sin, so, if sin was not restrained, it would immediately turn the soul into fiery oven, or a furnace of fire and brimstone.

7. It is no security to wicked men for one moment, that there are no visible means of death at hand. It is no security to a natural man, that he is now in health, and that he does not see which way he should now immediately go out of the world by any accident, and that there is no visible danger in any respect in his circumstances. The manifold and continual experience of the world in all ages shows this is no evidence, that a man is not on the very brink of eternity, and that the next step will not be into another world. The unseen, unthought of ways and means of persons going suddenly out of the world are innumerable and

inconceivable. Unconverted men walk over the pit of hell on a rotten covering, and there are innumerable places in this covering so weak that they will not bear their weight, and these places are not seen. The arrows of death fly unseen at noonday; the sharpest sight cannot discern them. God has so many different unsearchable ways of taking wicked men out of the world and sending them to hell, that there is nothing to make it appear, that God had need to be at the expense of a miracle, or go out of the ordinary course of his providence, to destroy any wicked man, at any moment. All the means that there are of sinners going out of the world, are so in God's hands, and so universally and absolutely subject to his power and determination, that it does not depend at all the less on the mere will of God, whether sinners shall at any moment go to hell, than if means were never made use of, or at all concerned in the case.

8. Natural men's prudence and care to preserve their own lives, or the care of others to preserve them, do not secure them a moment. To this, divine providence and universal experience do also bear testimony. There is this clear evidence that men's own wisdom is no security to them from death; that if it were otherwise we should see some difference between the wise and politic men of the world, and others, with regard to their liableness to early and unexpected death: but how is it in fact? Eccl. 2:16, "How dieth the wise man? even as the fool."

9. All wicked men's pains and *contrivance* which they use to escape hell, while they continue to reject Christ, and so remain wicked men, do not secure them from hell one moment. Almost every natural man that hears of hell, flatters himself that he shall escape it; he depends upon himself for his own security; he flatters himself in what he has done, in what he is now doing, or what he intends to do. Every one lays out matters in his own mind how he shall avoid damnation, and flatters himself that he contrives well for himself, and that his schemes will not fail. They hear

indeed that there are but few saved, and that the greater part of men that have died heretofore are gone to hell; but each one imagines that he lays out matters better for his own escape than others have done. He does not intend to come to that place of torment; he says within himself, that he intends to take effectual care, and to order matters so for himself as not to fail.

But the foolish children of men miserably delude themselves in their own schemes, and in confidence in their own strength and wisdom; they trust to nothing but a shadow. The greater part of those who heretofore have lived under the same means of grace, and are now dead, are undoubtedly gone to hell; and it was not because they were not as wise as those who are now alive: it was not because they did not lay out matters as well for themselves to secure their own escape. If we could speak with them, and inquire of them, one by one, whether they expected, when alive, and when they used to hear about hell, ever to be the subjects of misery: we doubtless, should hear one and another reply, "No, I never intended to come here: I had laid out matters otherwise in my mind; I thought I should contrive well for myself: I thought my scheme good. I intended to take effectual care; but it came upon me unexpected; I did not look for it at that time, and in that manner; it came as a thief: Death outwitted me: God's wrath was too quick for me. Oh, my cursed foolishness! I was flattering myself, and pleasing myself with vain dreams of what I would do hereafter; and when I was saying, Peace and safety, then sudden destruction came upon me."

10. God has laid himself under no *obligation*, by any promise to keep any natural man out of hell one moment. God certainly has made no promises either of eternal life, or of any deliverance or preservation from eternal death, but what are contained in the covenant of grace, the promises that are given in Christ, in whom all the promises are yea and amen. But surely they have no interest in the promises of the covenant of grace who are not the

children of the covenant, who do not believe in any of the promises, and have no interest in the Mediator of the covenant.

So that, whatever some have imagined and pretended about promises made to natural men's earnest seeking and knocking, it is plain and manifest, that whatever pains a natural man takes in religion, whatever prayers he makes, till he believes in Christ, God is under no manner of obligation to keep him a moment from eternal destruction.

So that, thus it is that natural men are held in the hand of God, over the pit of hell; they have deserved the fiery pit, and are already sentenced to it; and God is dreadfully provoked, his anger is as great towards them as to those that are actually suffering the executions of the fierceness of his wrath in hell, and they have done nothing in the least to appease or abate that anger, neither is God in the least bound by any promise to hold them up one moment; the devil is waiting for them, hell is gaping for them, the flames gather and flash about them, and would fain lay hold on them, and swallow them up; the fire pent up in their own hearts is struggling to break out: and they have no interest in any Mediator, there are no means within reach that can be any security to them. In short, they have no refuge, nothing to take hold of; all that preserves them every moment is the mere arbitrary will, and uncovenanted, unobliged forbearance of an incensed God.

APPLICATION

The use of this awful subject may be for awakening unconverted persons in this congregation. This that you have heard is the case of every one of you that are out of Christ.—That world of misery, that lake of burning brimstone, is extended abroad under you. There is the dreadful pit of the glowing flames of the wrath of God; there is hell's wide gaping mouth open; and you have nothing to stand upon, nor any thing to take hold of; there is nothing between you and hell but the air; it is only the power and mere pleasure of God that holds you up.

You probably are not sensible of this; you find you are kept out of hell, but do not see the hand of God in it; but look at other things, as the good state of your bodily constitution, your care of your own life, and the means you use for your own preservation. But indeed these things are nothing; if God should withdraw his hand, they would avail no more to keep you from falling, than the thin air to hold up a person that is suspended in it.

Your wickedness makes you as it were heavy as lead, and to tend downwards with great weight and pressure towards hell; and if God should let you go, you would immediately sink and swiftly descend and plunge into the bottomless gulf, and your healthy constitution, and your own care and prudence, and best contrivance, and all your righteousness, would have no more influence to uphold you and keep you out of hell, than a spider's web would have to stop a falling rock. Were it not for the sovereign pleasure of God, the earth would not bear you one moment; for you are a burden to it; the creation groans with you; the creature is made subject to the bondage of your corruption, not willingly; the sun does not willingly shine upon you to give you light to serve sin and Satan; the earth does not willingly yield her increase to satisfy your lusts; nor is it willingly a stage for your wickedness to be acted upon; the air does not willingly serve you for breath to maintain the flame of life in your vitals, while you spend your life in the service of God's enemies. God's creatures are good, and were made for men to serve God with, and do not willingly subserve to any other purpose, and groan when they are abused to purposes so directly contrary to their nature and end. And the world would spew you out, were it not for the sovereign hand of him who hath subjected it in hope. There are the black clouds of God's wrath now hanging directly over your heads, full of the dreadful storm, and big with thunder; and were it not for the restraining hand of God, it would immediately burst forth upon you. The sovereign pleasure of God, for the present, stays his rough wind; otherwise it would come with fury, and your destruction would come like a whirlwind, and you would be like the chaff of the summer threshing floor.

The wrath of God is like great waters that are dammed for the present; they increase more and more, and rise higher and higher, till an outlet is given; and the longer the stream is stopped, the more rapid and mighty is its course, when once it is let loose. It is true, that judgment against your evil works has not been executed hitherto; the floods of God's vengeance have been withheld; but your guilt in the mean time is constantly increasing, and you are every day treasuring up more wrath; the waters are constantly rising, and waxing more and more mighty; and there is nothing but the mere pleasure of God, that holds the waters back, that are unwilling to be stopped, and press hard to go forward. If God should only withdraw his hand from the floodgate, it would immediately fly open, and the fiery floods of the fierceness and wrath of God, would rush forth with inconceivable fury, and would come upon you with omnipotent power; and if your strength were ten thousand times greater than it is, yea, ten thousand times greater than the strength of the stoutest, sturdiest devil in hell, it would be nothing to withstand or endure it.

The bow of God's wrath is bent, and the arrow made ready on the string, and justice bends the arrow at your heart, and strains the bow, and it is nothing but the mere pleasure of God, and that of an angry God, without any promise or obligation at all, that keeps the arrow one moment from being made drunk with your blood. Thus all you that never passed under a great change of heart, by the mighty power of the Spirit of God upon your souls; all you that were never born again, and made new creatures, and raised from being dead in sin, to a state of new, and before altogether unexperienced light and life, are in the hands of

210

an angry God. However you may have reformed your life in many things, and may have had religious affections, and may keep up a form of religion in your families and closets, and in the house of God, it is nothing but his mere pleasure that keeps you from being this moment swallowed up in everlasting destruction. However unconvinced you may now be of the truth of what you hear, by and by you will be fully convinced of it. Those that are gone from being in the like circumstances with you, see that it was so with them; for destruction came suddenly upon most of them; when they expected nothing of it, and while they were saying, Peace and safety: now they see, that those things on which they depended for peace and safety, were nothing but thin air and empty shadows.

The God that holds you over the pit of hell, much as one holds a spider, or some loathsome insect over the fire, abhors you, and is dreadfully provoked: his wrath towards you burns like fire; he looks upon you as worthy of nothing else, but to be cast into the fire; he is of purer eyes than to bear to have you in his sight; you are ten thousand times more abominable in his eyes, than the most hateful venomous serpent is in ours. You have offended him infinitely more than ever a stubborn rebel did his prince; and yet it is nothing but his hand that holds you from falling into the fire every moment. It is to be ascribed to nothing else that you did not go to hell the last night; that you were suffered to awake again in this world, after you closed your eyes to sleep. And there is no other reason to be given, why you have not dropped into hell since you arose in the morning, but that God's hand has held you up. There is no other reason to be given why you have not gone to hell, since you have sat here in the house of God, provoking his pure eyes by your sinful wicked manner of attending his solemn worship. Yea, there is nothing else that is to be given as a reason why you do not this very moment drop down into hell.

O sinner! Consider the fearful danger you are in: it is a great furnace of wrath, a wide and bottomless pit, full of the fire of wrath, that you are held over in the hand of that God, whose wrath is provoked and incensed as much against you, as against many of the damned in hell. You hang by a slender thread, with the flames of divine wrath flashing about it, and ready every moment to singe it, and burn it asunder; and you have no interest in any Mediator, and nothing to lay hold of to save yourself, nothing to keep off the flames of wrath, nothing of your own, nothing that you ever have done, nothing that you can do, to induce God to spare you one moment.—And consider here more particularly,

1. *Whose* wrath it is: it is the wrath of the infinite God. If it were only the wrath of man, though it were of the most potent prince, it would be comparatively little to be regarded. The wrath of kings is very much dreaded, especially of absolute monarchs, who have the possessions and lives of their subjects wholly in their power, to be disposed of at their mere will. Prov. 20:2, "The fear of a king is as the roaring of a lion: Whoso provoketh him to anger, sinneth against his own soul." The subject that very much enrages an arbitrary prince is liable to suffer the most extreme torments that human art can invent, or human power can inflict. But the greatest earthly potentates in their greatest majesty and strength, and when clothed in their greatest terrors, are but feeble, despicable worms of the dust, in comparison of the great and almighty Creator and King of heaven and earth. It is but little that they can do, when most enraged, and when they have exerted the utmost of their fury. All the kings of the earth, before God, are as grasshoppers; they are nothing, and less than nothing: both their love and their hatred is to be despised. The wrath of the great King of kings is as much more terrible than theirs, as his majesty is greater. Luke 12:4-5, "And I say unto you, my friends, Be not afraid of them that kill the body, and after that, have no more that they can do. But I will

forewarn you whom you shall fear: Fear him, which after he hath killed, hath power to cast into hell: yea, I say unto you, Fear him."

2. It is the *fierceness* of his wrath that you are exposed to. We often read of the fury of God; as in Isa. 59:18, "According to their deeds, accordingly he will repay fury to his adversaries." So Isa. 66:15, "For behold, the Lord will come with fire, and with his chariots like a whirlwind, to render his anger with fury, and his rebuke with flames of fire." And in many other places. So, we read of Rev. 19:15, "the wine press of the fierceness and wrath of Almighty God." The words are exceeding terrible. If it had only been said, "the wrath of God," the words would have implied that which is infinitely dreadful: but it is "the fierceness and wrath of God." The fury of God! The fierceness of Jehovah! Oh, how dreadful that must be! Who can utter or conceive what such expressions carry in them! But it is also "the fierceness and wrath of *Almighty* God." As though there would be a very great manifestation of his almighty power in what the fierceness of his wrath should inflict, as though omnipotence should be as it were enraged, and exerted, as men are wont to exert their strength in the fierceness of their wrath. Oh! then, what will be the consequence! What will become of the poor worm that shall suffer it! Whose hands can be strong? And whose heart can endure? To what a dreadful, inexpressible, inconceivable depth of misery must the poor creature be sunk who shall be the subject of this!

Consider this, you that are here present, that yet remain in an unregenerate state. That God will execute the fierceness of his anger, implies, that he will inflict wrath without any pity. When God beholds the ineffable extremity of your case, and sees your torment to be so vastly disproportioned to your strength, and sees how your poor soul is crushed, and sinks down, as it were, into an infinite gloom; he will have no compassion upon you, he will not forbear the executions of his wrath, or in the least lighten his hand; there shall be no moderation or mercy, nor will

God then at all stay his rough wind; he will have no regard to your welfare, nor be at all careful lest you should suffer too much in any other sense, than only that you shall *not suffer beyond what strict justice requires.* Nothing shall be withheld, because it is so hard for you to bear. Ezek. 8:18, "Therefore will I also deal in fury; mine eye shall not spare, neither will I have pity; and though they cry in mine ears with a loud voice, yet I will not hear them." Now God stands ready to pity you; this is a day of mercy; you may cry now with some encouragement of obtaining mercy. But when once the day of mercy is past, your most lamentable and dolorous cries and shrieks will be in vain; you will be wholly lost and thrown away of God, as to any regard to your welfare. God will have no other use to put you to, but to suffer misery; you shall be continued in being to no other end; for you will be a vessel of wrath fitted to destruction; and there will be no other use of this vessel, but to be filled full of wrath. God will be so far from pitying you when you cry to him, that it is said he will only "laugh and mock," Prov. 1:25-26. etc.

How awful are those words, which are the words of the great God. Isa. 63:3, "I will tread them in mine anger, and will trample them in my fury, and their blood shall be sprinkled upon my garments, and I will stain all my raiment." It is perhaps impossible to conceive of words that carry in them greater manifestations of these three things, *viz.* contempt, and hatred, and fierceness of indignation. If you cry to God to pity you, he will be so far from pitying you in your doleful case, or showing you the least regard or favor, that instead of that, he will only tread you under foot. And though he will know that you cannot bear the weight of omnipotence treading upon you, yet he will not regard that, but he will crush you under his feet without mercy; he will crush out your blood, and make it fly, and it shall be sprinkled on his garments, so as to stain all his raiment. He will not only hate you, but he will have you in the utmost contempt: no place shall be thought fit for you, but under his feet to be trodden down as the mire of the streets.

3. The misery you are exposed to is that which God will inflict to that end, that he might show what that wrath of Jehovah is. God hath had it on his heart to show to angels and men, both how excellent his love is, and also how terrible his wrath is. Sometimes earthly kings have a mind to show how terrible their wrath is, by the extreme punishments they would execute on those that would provoke them. Nebuchadnezzar, that mighty and haughty monarch of the Chaldean empire, was willing to show his wrath when enraged with Shadrach, Meshech, and Abednego; and accordingly gave orders that the burning fiery furnace should be heated seven times hotter than it was before; doubtless, it was raised to the utmost degree of fierceness that human art could raise it. But the great God is also willing to show his wrath, and magnify his awful majesty and mighty power in the extreme sufferings of his enemies. Rom. 9:22, "What if God, willing to show his wrath, and to make his power known, endured with much longsuffering the vessels of wrath fitted to destruction?" And seeing this is his design, and what he has determined, even to show how terrible the unrestrained wrath, the fury and fierceness of Jehovah is, he will do it to effect. There will be something accomplished and brought to pass that will be dreadful with a witness. When the great and angry God hath risen up and executed his awful vengeance on the poor sinner, and the wretch is actually suffering the infinite weight and power of his indignation, then will God call upon the whole universe to behold that awful majesty and mighty power that is to be seen in it. Isa. 33:12-14, "And the people shall be as the burnings of lime, as thorns cut up shall they be burnt in the fire. Hear ye that are far off, what I have done; and ye that are near, acknowledge my might. The sinners in Zion are afraid; fearfulness hath surprised the hypocrites," etc.

Thus it will be with you that are in an unconverted state, if you continue in it; the infinite might, and majesty, and terribleness of the omnipotent God shall be magnified upon you, in the ineffable strength of your torments. You shall be tormented in the presence of the holy angels, and in the presence of the Lamb; and when you shall be in this state of suffering, the glorious inhabitants of heaven shall go forth and look on the awful spectacle, that they may see what the wrath and fierceness of the Almighty is; and when they have seen it, they will fall down and adore that great power and majesty. Isa. 66:23-24, "And it shall come to pass, that from one new moon to another, and from one sabbath to another, shall all flesh come to worship before me, saith the Lord. And they shall go forth and look upon the carcasses of the men that have transgressed against me; for their worm shall not die, neither shall their fire be quenched, and they shall be an abhorring unto all flesh."

4. It is *everlasting* wrath. It would be dreadful to suffer this fierceness and wrath of Almighty God one moment; but you must suffer it to all eternity. There will be no end to this exquisite horrible misery. When you look forward, you shall see a long forever, a boundless duration before you, which will swallow up your thoughts, and amaze your soul; and you will absolutely despair of ever having any deliverance, any end, any mitigation, any rest at all. You will know certainly that you must wear out long ages, millions of millions of ages, in wrestling and conflicting with this almighty merciless vengeance; and then when you have so done, when so many ages have actually been spent by you in this manner, you will know that all is but a point to what remains. So that your punishment will indeed be infinite. Oh, who can express what the state of a soul in such circumstances is! All that we can possibly say about it, gives but a very feeble, faint representation of it; it is inexpressible and inconceivable: for "who knows the power of God's anger?"

How dreadful is the state of those that are daily and hourly in the danger of this great wrath and infinite misery! But this is the dismal case of every soul in this congregation that has not been born again, however moral and strict, sober and religious, they may otherwise be. Oh that you would consider it, whether you be young or old! There is reason to think, that there are many in this congregation now hearing this discourse that will actually be the subjects of this very misery to all eternity. We know not who they are, or in what seats they sit, or what thoughts they now have. It may be they are now at ease, and hear all these things without much disturbance, and are now flattering themselves that they are not the persons, promising themselves that they shall escape. If we knew that there was one person, and but one, in the whole congregation, that was to be the subject of this misery, what an awful thing would it be to think of! If we knew who it was, what an awful sight would it be to see such a person! How might all the rest of the congregation lift up a lamentable and bitter cry over him! But, alas! Instead of one, how many is it likely will remember this discourse in hell? And it would be a wonder, if some that are now present should not be in hell in a very short time, even before this year is out. And it would be no wonder if some persons, that now sit here, in some seats of this meetinghouse, in health, quiet and secure, should be there before tomorrow morning. Those of you that finally continue in a natural condition that shall keep out of hell longest will be there in a little time! Your damnation does not slumber; it will come swiftly, and, in all probability, very suddenly upon many of you. You have reason to wonder that you are not already in hell. It is doubtless the case of some whom you have seen and known, that never deserved hell more than you, and that heretofore appeared as likely to have been now alive as you. Their case is past all hope; they are crying in extreme misery and perfect despair; but here you are in the land of the living and in the house of God, and have an opportunity

217

to obtain salvation. What would not those poor damned hopeless souls give for one day's opportunity such as you now enjoy!

And now you have an extraordinary opportunity, a day wherein Christ has thrown the door of mercy wide open, and stands in calling and crying with a loud voice to poor sinners; a day wherein many are flocking to him, and pressing into the kingdom of God. Many are daily coming from the east, west, north and south; many that were very lately in the same miserable condition that you are in, are now in a happy state, with their hearts filled with love to him who has loved them, and washed them from their sins in his own blood, and rejoicing in hope of the glory of God. How awful is it to be left behind at such a day! To see so many others feasting, while you are pining and perishing! To see so many rejoicing and singing for joy of heart, while you have cause to mourn for sorrow of heart, and howl for vexation of spirit! How can you rest one moment in such a condition? Are not your souls as precious as the souls of the people at Suffield, where they are flocking from day to day to Christ?

Are there not many here who have lived long in the world, and are not to this day born again? And so are aliens from the commonwealth of Israel, and have done nothing ever since they have lived, but treasure up wrath against the day of wrath? Oh, sirs, your case, in an especial manner, is extremely dangerous. Your guilt and hardness of heart is extremely great. Do you not see how generally persons of your years are passed over and left, in the present remarkable and wonderful dispensation of God's mercy? You had need to consider yourselves, and awake thoroughly out of sleep. You cannot bear the fierceness and wrath of the infinite God.—And you, young men, and young women, will you neglect this precious season which you now enjoy, when so many others of your age are renouncing all youthful vanities, and flocking to Christ? You especially have now an extraordinary opportunity; but if you neglect it, it will soon be with you as with those persons who spent all the precious days of youth in sin, and are now come to such a dreadful pass in blindness and hardness.—And you, children, who are unconverted, do not you know that you are going down to hell, to bear the dreadful wrath of that God, who is now angry with you every day and every night? Will you be content to be the children of the devil, when so many other children in the land are converted, and are become the holy and happy children of the King of kings?

And let every one that is yet out of Christ, and hanging over the pit of hell, whether they be old men and women, or middle aged, or young people, or little children, now hearken to the loud calls of God's word and providence. This acceptable year of the Lord, a day of such great favor to some, will doubtless be a day of as remarkable vengeance to others. Men's hearts harden, and their guilt increases apace at such a day as this, if they neglect their souls; and never was there so great danger of such persons being given up to hardness of heart and blindness of mind. God seems now to be hastily gathering in his elect in all parts of the land; and probably the greater part of adult persons that ever shall be saved, will be brought in now in a little time, and that it will be as it was on the great outpouring of the Spirit upon the Jews in the apostles' days; the election will obtain, and the rest will be blinded. If this should be the case with you, you will eternally curse this day, and will curse the day that ever you was born, to see such a season of the pouring out of God's Spirit, and will wish that you had died and gone to hell before you had seen it. Now undoubtedly it is, as it was in the days of John the Baptist, the axe is in an extraordinary manner laid at the root of the trees, that every tree which brings not forth good fruit, may be hewn down and cast into the fire.

Therefore, let every one that is out of Christ, now awake and fly from the wrath to come. The wrath of Almighty God is now undoubtedly hanging over a great part of this congregation. Let every one fly out of Sodom:

"Haste and escape for your lives, look not behind you, escape to the mountain, lest you be consumed."